The Centurion

Veils of Truth

Brantley Loomis

Dedication

For Merlin the Meowser

Acknowledgment

I want to offer my sincere gratitude to everyone who helped me write this book.

About the Author

Brantley Loomis was educated at Lewis Clark State College in Lewiston, Idaho. He now makes his home in the Palouse region of Eastern Washington, where he lives with his wife and three children. Besides working on his next project, he is a technology evangelist, think tank, and implementer.

Preface

The good times were coming to an end. The evil spirit could not stand to see humanity happy and began conspiring against it as the power of the Guardian weakened. Soon, the world descended into chaos. Nobody was spared – including baby Madeline, who lost her parents to a violent attack soon after she was born.

Despite her tragic beginnings, she grew up to an astute and positive person, which was thanks in part to Karen – who took up the role of raising Madeline. Because of her resilient and honest personality, the ailing Guardian spirit decided to bestow Madeline with its powers. The evil, knowing this, decides to intervene so it can take over the world.

What follows is a thrilling story where the Guardian and evil spirit compete over Madeline, each trying to win her over. Caught in between, Madeline becomes excessively turbulent. Will she be able to overcome the evil spirit's temptations and remain eligible for receiving the Guardian's power? More importantly, how will she do this?

We all wonder if we are gifted or not.

Contents

Page Left Blank Intentionally

Chapter 1
Sunrise, Storm, and Lightning

'Finish off the red army.' Relaxing on his comfortable bed, the notorious dictator heard a voice coming from inside of him. He summoned his army within an hour and commanded them to expand to the east to eliminate the red army.

The greatest war of the time had commenced, turning the prosperous planet into a war zone. It was led by the kings, dictators, and leaders who considered themselves autonomous and independent, fighting to become the only supreme power on earth. Little did they know that their sovereignty was fake and illusionary. They were merely the puppets of a mischievous power that was whispering and imparting his evil wishes into their heedless minds.

During that turbulent time, on a bright sunny day, a baby with rosy cheeks was born. Her parents, Alton and Freya, were over the moon after being blessed with a daughter who looked like a little fairy. Alton was a government lawyer, living with his wife and baby in a beautiful town in southwest England. They lived in Glastonbury. The city only had a population of nine thousand people. The place was home for them. It was a beautiful place, and it was calm and peaceful there. Like most of the houses in Glastonbury, their house was a small one with three rooms in it. They had a small lawn in the front yard where Freya grew carrots and cucumber.

"I have discovered that a brutal force is planning to invade this town in a few days," Alton informed his wife, who was gently patting her five-day-old baby.

"Jesus! What are we going to do then?" Freya was shocked by the news. She had never imagined that they would have to leave the town one day.

"Don't worry, honey, our army is here. Numerous American soldiers are appointed." He tried to comfort his wife and added, *"We have been asked to leave for Wales within two days. I have learned that highways are blocked; therefore, it won't be convenient to travel by car. I have confirmed our train tickets for tomorrow. Get to packing at once and only bring essentials."*

"Absolutely," Freya replied.

The next morning, the family left for the station at dawn. By the time they reached and found their seats on the train, the sun was rising between the green hills, converting the dark black sky into bright blue. The birds were singing melodiously outside the window of their berth. The air was so clear that no one could anticipate the impending storm.

"I don't think I have seen a morning more beautiful than this," Alton commented, witnessing the enchanting view of the sunrise.

"You are right; it looks amazing," Freya seconded her husband.

The family was sitting in the business class berth of the train. Their one-week-old newborn was sleeping in her cart, wrapped in a pink fur blanket. The train was supposed to leave within ten minutes. There were passengers still rushing in, looking for their seats. An old couple entered their berth.

"Young man, can you help us with our luggage?" Dragging in their luggage, the older man asked Alton.

"Oh, yes, sure!" Alton got up from his seat and pushed their luggage under their seats.

"God bless you, my child," the old man was grateful.

"My name is George Smith, she is my wife Ruth Smith," Mr. Smith introduced themselves. He further added that he and his wife made Christmas ornaments.

That sounded interesting, mainly because Alton had never met a person before whose gift was such a profession. His wife, Mrs. Smith, also looked gentle yet mysterious. She was carrying a bible in one hand and a fruit basket in the other. It seemed the more the husband liked talking, the more his wife preferred keeping silent. Alton introduced themselves as well.

"You both make a beautiful couple," Mr. Smith commented.

"Thank you, Sir. Are you also going to Wales?" Alton asked.

"No, we will get off at Bristol," replied Mr. Smith and looked at the newborn.

"Hey, little kid," he leaned in and peered at the baby.

"How old is this angel?" Asked Mr. Smith.

"One week," Freya replied.

"O' my granddaughter is probably one week old too, we are going to Bristol to see her. My daughter-in-law lives there," the excitement to see his granddaughter was evident in the old man's voice.

"What about your son?" Freya could not help asking.

"My son," the old man paused. *"James was a soldier...he lost his life while serving on the border last month."*

It took him a while to say that. Freya and Alton saw tears rolling down his cheeks. Mrs. Smith patted on her husband's hand. Her eyes were teary too.

"I'm sorry," said Freya, who was now regretting her question.

"Don't be, my child. I'm sure our son is resting in peace in heaven," Mrs. Smith finally said something. Her voice was soft and warm.

Freya held the old lady's hand in hers and said, *"I'm sure he is,"* to which Mrs. Smith smiled gently.

Sleeping in her pram, the newborn woke up by the voices and started crying. Freya took her out of the pram and tried to divert her attention with the keys in her hand, which she had purposefully taken out from her pocket, but the baby would not stay quiet.

"Give her to me," Mrs. Smith extended her arms. The baby stopped crying as soon as Mrs. Smith held her in her arms.

The train started moving forward, and the golden sun started coming up. Its golden rays penetrated in the glass of the window and landed on the baby's rosy cheeks.

"Your child is blessed by the deities of heaven. She is the chosen one. Soon, she will be doing great things," Mrs. Smith forecasted, lovingly gazing at the newborn.

"What do you mean?" enquired Freya.

"Your daughter - I see a magical spark in her eyes. She is sent to stop an impending disaster," the old lady said with confidence.

Freya grinned on Mrs. Smith's innocence. She thought it was just another irrational thing that the elders would say. She was, however, amused by her daughter's smile, which she gave when Mrs. Smith tried to play with her cheeks. It was the first time she saw her daughter smile. As she smiled, the sun outside the window shined brighter.

The train had built the pace. It was leaving behind England and the times Alton and Freya had spent there. Though they were trying to look normal, it was tough for them to leave the place they had got emotionally attached to. It was around four years ago when they moved to England. They were newly married back then. If it were not the cataclysmic war, which had divided Europe by an iron curtain, they probably would have never left England. The war had not divided Europe only, but also the world. The year of 2187 was coming to an end, and the New Year seemingly was bringing a lot of destruction with it. Every nation was fighting a battle not only to serve their national interests but to take other nations to extinction. They said it was the war of ideology.

But the difference of ideology had existed since forever. They said it was a nuclear war. But they were completely aware of the disastrous consequences of nuclear weapons. They also said it was the space race that had divided the planet. But they were too naïve to understand there was no good in exploring space when their mother planet was crying for their attention and kindness. The logical minds were unable to understand the cause of the war. It seemed that all causes were merely built up by a higher power – a power invisible to human eyes, a power that wanted destruction, a power that asked for bloodshed only, a power that augmented the cruelty of leaders, a power that enjoyed the helplessness of innocent humans who had to leave their generations-old family homes.

What was that power? Why was it after the earth and its people? Why was it using the leaders and dictators to serve its objectives? Was that power inalienable? Was there anyone who could challenge that power? There was no one who could. It was taking the world to the height of annihilation and yet seemed unstoppable.

Looking around, Alton noticed most of the men on the train looked unhappy as if they were traveling against their wish to protect their family. Alton himself was a husband and now a father. He could completely relate to the anxiousness evident on the faces of those men. Alton sighed in grief and looked at his wife, who was sleeping on his shoulder. He fondly looked at her for a while. His gaze further traveled to his newborn's cart. His daughter's spotless face melted Alton's heart.

Remembering Mrs. Smith's words about her daughter possessing supernatural power, he also smiled like his wife. He thought anyone who saw his daughter's pure face would assume that. He realized that his child was too flawless to be going through this arduous journey just a week after her birth. However, there was nothing he could do but take her to a safer place.

The old couple was asleep too. Alton spotted grief on their faces. He cursed the war once more and silently wished the old couple patience and courage. He also wished no other parents should lose their child as they did. As Alton was about to fall asleep, the next station had arrived. The voices outside the station refrained him from falling asleep.

He looked around through the window to see which station it was but did not get a hint. After about 5 minutes, the train started moving again. As the train rebuilt its pace, it thundered outside. Alton noticed dark clouds rushing in on the clear sky. He felt his seat trembling as if the weighty clouds had entered the train as well. He turned around, looked back in the corridor, and saw a group of people wearing strange outfits running inside from the other corner.

They were countless and ruthless, destroying everything

that came in their way. Freya and the old couple woke up by the voices.

"Dearest God, what is happening?" Mrs. Smith was the first one to react.

"Pirates have boarded the train; please run to the other corner," Alton caught in a state of catatonic oblivion, finally lurched into action in the last second. Freya immediately took out her baby from her pram. Alton paved ways for the old couple to pass and asked his wife to follow them.

"Please be quick honey, they are almost here," Alton was shivering. He had never encountered such a situation before. It was so hard for him to figure out what to do. The monsters reached them. They grabbed Alton from his collar and pulled him back. One of them punched Alton on his face. He fell and moaned.

"Bastard!" He said, spitting on Alton.

"Alton!" Holding her baby, Freya cried.

"Please stop that!" Mr. Smith came forward to stop them. They hit Mr. Smith and asked Mrs. Smith for their money and gold.

Alton and Freya could not believe when they saw the pirates stabbing the old couple when they got nothing valuable from them. They got worried and feared for the life of their one-week-old. Freya's grip on her baby became stronger. Alton grabbed his wife, and insanely ran in the opposite direction. They stopped when they found a corner to hide.

"Honey, run to the end of the train and find a hiding spot for yourself and our baby...until then, I will try to distract them," Alton instructed his wife.

"I cannot leave you," Freya resisted.

"Please Frey, understand what I'm saying, they will be here any minute, please save yourself and our baby, I'm coming after you," Alton insisted. *"Run, Frey!"* he insisted.

Freya kissed her husband with teary eyes and ran toward the end of the train. Alton closed his eyes and tried to store enough energy to fight against the devils who were killing the passengers as if they were mere toys. He heard the cries of hundreds of passengers being agonized and murdered by that barbaric group.

Alton never knew what it felt like being a father until his baby was born. He did not get amazed when he saw those fathers on the train, sacrificing their lives for their children because he knew he, too, would do that to save his family. When the marauders were about to reach Alton, a massive storm came upon the train. Thunder crashed outside. Alton felt a storm build inside him as well. His emotions to save his family had reached the peak. Alton felt gale in his gut and thunders in his mind. The uproar of his heart provided him strength. The internal fury was harmonizing with the storm outside.

As a result, Alton kicked one of the pirates with great force as soon as he tried to attack him. He hit many others who came his way. He was surprised by his brawn. He looked at the sky through the window. It was raining. Tears of gratitude flowed from his eyes as well. The group realized his strength and decided to strike together. On one side, it was Alton alone, blocking their way to the next railcars of the train; on the other side, it was the barbaric group glaring at the young man who had become an albatross around their neck. They jointly set on Alton, pushing him down and hitting him with the weapons they carried. They beat him until he succumbed. They left him there and rushed forward to the next railcars. They looted and killed every passenger they came across.

Freya, who had hidden herself with her baby in the last railcar, realized it would not take them long to reach there. She took a good look at her baby and carefully strapped her on a seat. She kissed her rosy cheeks and went to face the pirates alone to keep her baby safe. She looked around the railcar; there was no one who could help her.

"Alton, where are you?" She whispered.

Though she somehow knew that her husband had sacrificed his life while protecting them. Freya gasped at her helplessness yet moved forward to find a way out. Despite being careful, the pirates saw her when she reached the second last railcar. When they were about to leap to her, Freya saw the coupler.

In a split second, she decided to unhitch the railcar. She hurried to the coupler and started opening it. The pirates pulled her hair, but she did not move an inch, her hands still opening the coupler. They stabbed her in the back. Freya groaned in pain, yet she chose not to quit. Finally, she opened the coupler, and the last railcar got unhitched. The train moved forward, leaving behind the detached railcar. Freya looked at the railcar, which had her baby, and took her last breath. It became dark. There were flashes of lightning and uproars of thunder. The baby in the railcar cried at the top of her lungs. The wind whipped around the railcar, ebbing and flowing into a force that pushed hard. Slowly gaining momentum that carried the baby back to the nearest city, the railcar came to a stop short of the terminal, and the baby was crying loudly.

Merlin, the cat, emerged from the weeds and strolled towards the noise. Soon the cat was upon a local woman named Karen walking to her home. The cat winded its way around her legs and meowed loudly. Karen looked down and saw the cat's ears twitching and trying to focus on something. The wind died down, and now Karen heard the cries of the baby.

"What is this noise?" Asking herself, she turned around and tried to trace the cries.

She saw a railcar standing on the railway track. She went inside and found a baby more beautiful than stars.

"Whose baby is this?" When she reached home, she was asked by her neighbor. To which Karen replied:

"She is my baby, Madeline."

Chapter 2
Candle Light

The power of light and the prophecy of protection were all composed in an entity known to be the Guardian. The Guardian was not a person but a state that was not dependent on an individual, but a legacy that was to remain till the end of time. The right candidate was to be guided, protected, and prepared before the prophecy was declared to the person.

The Guardian had lived for thousands of years and had seen the world evolve tremendously. It had seen man traveling on foot, barely covering up his body with leaves. It had seen men eat raw food and be handicapped of communication. The world was a different place centuries ago. It was slow and purposeless, and like how the days and nights have been constant since the existence of the human race, so has the entity of the Guardian.

This was the first time the Guardian was to pass its powers and responsibilities to another human after thousands of years. It couldn't just be randomly passed on to any individual, as there came immense responsibility with the power. After all, the fate of humanity was at stake. The potential candidates for the prophecy had to undergo a series of tests to determine whether or not they were worthy of the role. The most important element was purity. The potential candidate had to depict a level of purity for the Guardianship to be relinquished for the person. The time had come for the transfer of Guardian's powers to the worthy. The mystic powers needed an heir, and the last job of the Guardian was to find that person before the end of its cycle.

The life of the current Guardian was coming to an end. No one is meant to live forever, and the case with the Guardian was no different. Before the life cycle of the Guardian came to an end, the next Guardian was to be prepared and embedded with the powers. This was done to ensure the next chosen one carried out their job justly.

Madeline was the next Guardian. The little angel illuminated her surroundings since the day she was born. The light was always around her, whether inside her eyes or around her soul. Her smile was bright, as bright as the first ray of light in a dark night of sadness. Her face shone like the morning spring sun. She was to replace the Guardian; she was to be the next Guardian. It was only a matter of time.

The day she turned a hundred and one years old, Madeline was to die and become the Guardian. Death was only a new beginning. Madeline was not the first person to be chosen as the Guardian. There were many selected before her. They either lacked purity or had the characteristic traits of misusing the powers. With omnipotence came great responsibility, and if that responsibility was not acknowledged, it could lead to disasters. As the guardian existed, so did the evil. If the wrong person was chosen, the imbalance created by the excess of evil could alter the entire human system that had evolved for centuries to get to its current state.

The search was not limited to one region. Across the seven oceans, from small islands to populated societies, the Guardian searched for the righteous heir everywhere. It did find a few potential prospects, but they either lacked the strength or were unable to clear the test for one reason or the other. It had monitored and observed the traits of the candidate. It also tried to guide newborn babies as there was no man as pure as them. It used its powers to protect them, but they never seemed to appear fit for the role.

There were times when the training yielded satisfactory outcomes, but the genetic inheritance turned out to be the barrier. Certain specific characteristics possessed by the chosen baby marked her unsafe before adopting those powers. Madeline, however, was different. Since the moment she was born, her eyes held a pure light, unlike any the Guardian had ever seen in its search. Her genes were independent of any destructive traits, and her eyes were that of a leader, a responsible leader who had the capability to combat against any evil. It was still a long way to go, and only time could unveil her destiny.

There were a lot of factors that were to be considered, from family background and sense of responsibility to likeness and biases. The reason behind focusing on little things was because they held equal importance when gauged in contrast to the bigger ones. Every aspect of the person's reality, being chosen, was to be brought under consideration. The strengths could be modified, but the capacity to understand and act under the interest of righteousness was the most critical component the Guardian sought. Madeline had that component.

Madeline was coming from a war-torn region. Her parents had never done injustice to anyone. They had never taken ill advantage of any situation. The vision the old lady had on the train, and the way she had survived were all linked to a bigger purpose. It justified how Madeline was going to be a strong woman who had the potential to become the next Guardian. She was coming from difficult circumstances, and since the departure of her family, she was to be groomed by someone else and not her mother. The journey was going to be difficult with a naturally resilient attitude. She was by far the best candidate.

People who live in ideal conditions, having a comfortable environment and family to cherish are more likely to take advantage of their blessings. They are more likely to not value the responsibility bestowed upon them in comparison to the ones who have had sufferings. The innocent little child, Madeline, had a dark beginning to her life. Her losses indicated that the capabilities she would comprise of facing difficulties would indeed be commendable. It is nature's way of maintaining its balance.

The need for good will always be there until evil exists, and it always does. There was a reason why the Guardian existed, and that reason was undoubtedly the existence of evil. The mischievous power was evil. He was insidious and had evil plans to cause people pain and misery. There was nothing virtuous he had within himself; everything about him was unjust.

The evil was aware of the Guardian's plans. The Guardian had always been an obstacle in his path, bringing unrest and chaos. He knew that the Guardian's cycle was coming to an end and that it was looking for an heir to transfer its powers. From his perspective, it was essentially an opportunity for him to stop the Guardian from grooming a new person for the role. If he got successful in halting the Guardian from doing so, the atrocities it conspired for were all going to come to fruition.

He was aiding the war and enlarging its impact as it knew that it was the only way it could get rid of the potential prospect that was to become the new Guardian. Little did he know that it was going to work the other way round. He was a combination of all the evils, and his entire focus centered on pleasing his Master. Like him, his Master also had evil plans, which were only to be accomplished if the Guardian was taken out of the equation.

The battle between him and the Guardian could only come to an end if either of them was eliminated. Good and evil, despite being opposites, cater to each other's existence. If the Guardian ended up on the losing side, the world was to be a place where living and inhibiting was next to impossible, and within a matter of few days, the entire race of humankind was to fall apart. The Guardian had to stop him from doing so. So far, it had been successful, but this was the most critical phase. If the power was not transferred to the best individual, the evil would take control of everything and would rule the world along with his Master. The war had taken away plenty of lives, including Madeline's family. Madeline was the target; in fact, everybody on the train was so that there was no person available for the Guardian to train.

He couldn't have known that the adorable baby girl traveling in that train was to be selected by the Guardian as the person to take its powers. He had made things easier for the Guardian as Madeline did not have a family and was sub-consciously gaining strength. That's what tough circumstances do; they either weaken you or make you stronger. In Madeline's case, it served as a source of strength. He, too, had lived for thousands of years. He and the Guardian knew a great deal about themselves. Over the course of time, they had developed an understanding of each other's tactics and strategies.

One knew how the other functioned. The Guardian knew that he was responsible for the war and that he was trying to take away all innocent lives of the region. If it weren't for Madeline's mother, he would have succeeded. If anyone were to adopt the mystic powers, he and his Master would have to wait for another cycle. They had waited very long for this cycle to complete and had to stop the transfer this time; otherwise, their goals were to be unachievable for at least the next thousand years. He knew that the Guardian would not transfer the powers to anyone weak.

The only option they were left with was to eliminate any potential person living, with regard to the fact that the Guardian was to protect her through her powers. As a baby, Madeline was unaware of the purpose and the position awaiting her. Although, she was already given enough forces to defend herself from the evil power. A baby does not need to do much to make a place into people's hearts, but Madeline was special. The light that she exhaled out was indeed transpiring. She had the power of light - the 'aurora.' That power enhanced her capability to get deep into the hearts of people she had around her. Even if the people around her did not pay attention to her, she would only need a few moments to grab their attention through her beauty and luminousness compounded within her soul. Her sharp, bright features created affection among anybody that looked at her for even a moment. Unbeknown, the child in need of protection, was to become the protector herself.

The candlelight casting a shadow is weak and flickers from the blowing wind. Just like the candle, Madeline too faltered. She was young and vulnerable, and the wind ambled blowing over her was making her flicker. It was the job of the Guardian to ensure that the wind was unable to blow the candle out.

The candle brings light into places surrounded by darkness; there are many candles, but not all tend to resist heavy winds coming their way. Those winds can easily take the light away from the candle. But if the candle is surrounded by palms, no matter how intense the winds are, they are only to reflect away, while the candle stays lit. Madeline was that candle.

Under the rain of time, Karen acted as the umbrella shielding Madeline while she gradually grew closer to her destiny. Karen gave her all the love and affection a mother could. She admired Madeline as a child, took great care of her, and provided for her the best she could in her capacity. She took great care of her. Even though Madeline was not born from her womb, she treated her like her own blood.

"Do you know what happens when you cry?" Karen would usually say to Madeline whenever she found her crying. She would only freeze her eyes at her mother to hear the same thing she always said.

"It makes mommy sad. Do you want mommy to be sad?" hearing this, Madeline would smile at Karen and stop crying.

Madeline had developed a strong bond with her mother. They appeared different, Karen had big hazel colored eyes that beautifully complimented the other features of her face. She was short of stature and had blonde hair. She had a deep, meaningful voice. Madeline, on the other hand, had beautiful eyes, shaped as if Leonardo Da Vinci's painted them. Her voice had politeness that depicted control being soft at the same time.

She had dark brown hair and was taller from the other children of her age. Madeline always adored her mother and wanted to be like her. She dearly loved Karen. Karen had sensed that there was something extraordinary about her adopted child. There was extra calmness and composure in her, unlike kids of her age.

Also, Karen noticed that there was something that was protecting her. She never saw her little girl trip while learning to walk. She was amused to see her start walking without any help and without ever failing. Failure is not a bad thing, and if someone exempted from experiencing it at any level, there is undoubtedly something supernatural about it.

When Karen saw her walking for the first time, she was stunned to see the balance she maintained. Karen wondered if there was something special about her family, which she had never met. She wondered if Madeline's family had God-gifted strengths. There was something exceptional about her adopted daughter.

"My princess, Mommy loves you," were the first words that came out of her mouth.

Karen had developed a strong attachment to her. She found joy in taking care of the little angel who was steadily growing. With the Guardian's secret help, it was all the easier to take care of Madeline. There were a few moments when she thought that it wasn't just her strengths that kept her safe; she assumed it was God that looked after her. She felt so because she had adopted her with honest intentions, and she loved her with all her heart.

It was impossible for anybody to say that Madeline was an adopted child and not Karen's, well neither did anyone know. Madeline started speaking late. She was around three years old when she started talking, but yet again, surprisingly, Madeline spoke fluently from the day she started speaking. Her speech was audible and clear. The vocabulary she had was of a seven-year-old or older.

Karen was stunned. One thing after another about her adopted child would lead her to disbelief. Her voice had the childish elements of sound frequencies, but the clarity and explanation with which she communicated were by far phenomenal. By the time she turned five, she was capable of sewing. Karen only gave her a few lessons, that too on her insistence when she saw her mother stitch. She started doing it herself, and as Karen would say to her, *"You have amazing hands,"* to which she would return her a graceful smile. Karen did not know that she was not the only teacher Madeline had. The Guardian had powers to manipulate nature. Once Madeline tripped over a stone. Rather than hitting her head on the tree that was right in front of her, she missed it and fell over to the side, saving herself.

Karen was pulling water out of the river, which is why she did not notice. When they got home, Madeline told her what happened. Karen got worried and started examining her forehead, and to her surprise, she did not even spot a single scar or wound in any part of her face. She was thinking of her as a child and ignored what Madeline said.

Things kept on happening, and Karen kept on ignoring. She believed her to be a God-gifted child and did not discuss the stories she shared of her experiences, pretending it all to be normal. No one in the town knew that she wasn't her child. The war wasn't over. It wasn't to be unless the devil and his master were successful in holding the Guardian to transcend its powers. Since Madeline was a child without a father, Karen felt it was her responsibility to protect her from harm's way. She also had to play the role of her father and make sure she did not miss her presence. *"I will always be here for you,"* she would often say, kissing her forehead. Madeline never felt bullied. It's not that no one made attempts to intimidate her, but all those attempts went in vain because of how the Guardian protected her. The malicious power was very influential, and he could easily convince people to do the wrong. He would often influence the kids that lived nearby to bully her. Somehow Karen would always be around whenever a kid intended to do so. Kids were easily convinced to get after the girl who did not have a father. But the Guardian would bring up a reason to get Karen there, and she would then take control of the situation, keeping her safe from all the bullies that confronted her.

Even if Karen were unable to get there, the Guardian would figure a way out to get the kids away. Once she was out playing in the field when a bunch of teenage kids approached her because of the mischievous power's influence. As they got closer to her, they spotted a dog running their way. The dogs ignored Madeline running behind the boys, chasing them off. She felt awkward the first time and noticed that she always got help when she needed it. She was too young to understand where she was getting help from, and thinking about being protected by the Guardian was way beyond her imagination. She walked home, thinking about all the events and decided to discuss it with her mother. It was too much for a six-year-old to comprehend. Karen did not pay much attention to her incubations about always getting help, but got more focused on her safety. She knew that it wasn't safe for her to roam around.

Already the war was a source of great fear, and even though she had not gone far from the house, she was given further instructions always to stay close to Karen. Karen knew she couldn't always have Madeline right next to her. The thoughts of getting her harmed were clouding in her head. All she could do was keep her close and pray for the war to get over as soon as possible.

The Guardian was looking after her, and if Karen had the slightest of a hint, her stress levels would have gone really down. Madeline was safe, though she was always under an evil threat. The Guardian was committed to keeping her away from trouble. The Guardian was watering the seed until it could be harvested for a higher purpose beyond human strengths and imagination.

Chapter 3
Dark Chocolate

The war seemed never-ending. Every passing day made living conditions miserable. The entire region was affected, and every person living in that region was under threat. Karen always looked at Madeline as her daughter. She had developed a bond with her that she had even forgotten that Madeline wasn't her biological daughter but someone who was adopted. Karen was very concerned about Madeline's safety. She wanted to keep her as safe as she possibly could, which is why she always kept a close eye on her.

She did not allow her to go out more often, and being a little child, all Madeline could do was agree. Madeline was a sweet child. She never rebelled against Karen, and things between the two were always calm. Madeline loved her foster mother exactly how she would have loved her birth mother as Karen's love was as much as it is of any mother toward her biological child. With the region getting more unsafe by the day, Karen decided to move her to a private school where she would be safe. It was hard to predict when the war was to get over, but until that was happening, she had to find her daughter a safer place. Since the town had become a dangerous place, Madeline mostly stayed at home, which is why her learning process abruptly paused at an age when learning is very critical.

She needed that learning as it was to transform her into a well-mannered lady, the kind every mother wishes to see her daughter as. There was a town nearby unaffected by the war. Karen got Madeline admitted to a private school in the city that was hardly twenty miles away from Karen's house. Private schools were rigorous, and Karen did not know about that. Even if she did, there wasn't much she could have done.

Karen raised Madeline with a lot of love and sincere gratitude. Ending up in a strict school without being monitored by her only parent was too much to ask from a young child. But she wasn't an ordinary child, and there was something special about her. Her smile reflected composure, and her eyes displayed strength. There was something about her that consistently expressed how protected and loved she was by God and His angels. Looking at her, Karen would get confidence and trust in God that there is nothing that could happen to her and that she was in this world for a reason. Only time was to tell.

Things were challenging at her new school. Students punished for the slightest of mistakes they made. Even if they were five minutes late to get to the class, they are put in detention. Other things like bringing a wrong notebook or not covering her mouth while yawning and similar little reasons would not go by unattended. She would get punished for the slightest mistake she made, and the concept of accepting apologies seemed non-existent.

This aggressive attitude of the teachers was turning Madeline into someone rebellious, unlike who she truly was. At times, she did not even know what mistake she made and would take her punishment. With the increasing punishments, her sense of guilt was dying out, and why wouldn't it? She was not told where she was wrong most of the time, which is why there was a sense of hate developing in her. That hate was not mainly against a teacher or a student but was against the system imposed on her.

Though the unfairness or a rather over-strict environment was getting onto her, her consciousness had not registered the rebellion growing inside of her. Karen was trying to settle down in the town, which is why she wasn't able to notice the changing behavior of Madeline. When Madeline was home, she was calm and relaxed. She would be Karen's tail and went with her wherever she did. Karen thought it was because of the new environment; little did she know about how things were progressing in school. The Guardian was very sick. She was trying to recuperate and get back into a position from where she could complete her quest to transfer the legacy. The Guardian had grown old and tired. The sickness had weakened her powers. She was unable to look over Madeline and protect her. Madeline left on her own.

Unable to adjust to the new environment, Madeline was struggling to keep up with the school. Madeline was a brilliant student. She was quick at grasping concepts and could relate science to her everyday life. Injustice, what it was in her eyes, was the only de-motivating factor. The mischievous power had realized that the Guardian wasn't doing well. It was like an opportunity coming of a time bracket that was independent of the Guardian's interference.

He couldn't have wished for a better opportunity. He knew how school was tampering Madeline's personality, and all that happened was to trigger her sub-consciousness to alter her mindset and let her character develop destructively. Madeline had formulated a concept that said no matter what she did, the punishment was inevitable. The demon was smart to manipulate this perception and used his powers to influence the brats of the school, dictating them to get close to Madeline and involve her in all the indecent activities they performed.

Karen had taught Madeline to live by the rules and walk the straight and narrow discipline. Gradually, school life had drawn her distant from Karen's designed principles, and she had become willing to test her limits and ignore all the rules that were structured by her mother for her.

She was put on detention regularly. Madeline started being more careless, which led her to make more mistakes. She was least concerned about time and had no hesitations to confront her teachers even when she was at fault. All her friends were students who were rebellious and spent most of their time in school detention. The impact and influence of the company are limitless for people of any age, but the younger the child, the stronger are the chances of him/her to come under the control, so was the case with Madeline. Bunking classes had become her routine. There wasn't any specific reason behind skipping classes besides to please her friends and spend time with them. The teachers always gave her a tough time, which is why making a decision that took her away from them, was most likely going to attract her.

Once, she was in class, while all her friends were outside. As soon as she found herself a chair and settled down, her newly made friends who were influenced by the demon invited her to skip her class and join them outside. She had just gotten in, and getting out of the class was an impossible task. In a class of fewer than thirty students, it was extremely difficult to exit the class without getting into the teacher's sight.

If Madeline was caught making a move in an attempt to exit, severe punishment would ensue. The peers waiting outside the class were always communicating with her through gestures, asking her to leave. She thought it over, and when she realized there wasn't a way she could sneak out, she picked up her bag and ran outside the door without turning back and hid in a secretive place that only her friends knew about.

After running from the class right in front of the teacher, she realized that going back to class was inviting trouble. So she decided never to attend it. One class after another, she started bunking all her classes, and this also meant receiving detention or punishments. Karen would drop her at the school gate, she would walk inside, and without going to the class, she would walk directly toward the meeting area.

The school was of a decent size, their secret meeting area was away from the classroom, around the play area. There was a room for the school guard who lived there and would be out in the daytime. The brats would occupy the space behind his office, and since nobody was able to see them there, they sat there for hours and would leave when it was time to go home.

There were hardly a couple of classes she attended in a week, and even in those classes, her attitude toward her teachers had changed from being defensive and soft-spoken to offensive and aggressive. She became more arrogant than the rest of the bunch she stayed accompanied to. She would interfere in lessons and would answer back to teachers. She did not feel scared to get punished; instead, she considered it a reward and a symbol of bravery. She used to be very embarrassed when she first arrived at school and during her punishment. With time, proudness replaced embarrassment. The first time a child develops a sense of peer pressure, he/she only interprets the right as something that makes the peers happy. In striving to satisfy them, no limitations or boundaries exist. The appreciation received from the peers is unmatchable even if it was morally incorrect. Madeline was willing to cross every line to make sure her peers were happy with her. She did not know who the evil power was or how he was manipulating the bunch of kids that she thought were her friends. She lacked the Guardian's help and assistance without knowing she ever had it. Since Karen was the only person she had at home, she relied heavily on her newly made friendships and was not willing to lose them at any cost.

If she had more options and attracted by a decent company, she wouldn't have become what she had. She did not know that an evil power existed that had targeted her, and neither did she know that the Guardian existed, who had found Madeline to be the chosen one. Karen was unaware of her activities at school. She was involved in her new life and was trying to settle down with her new job and the environment. It's not that she wasn't concerned, and since she believed that she was going to a strict school, she only felt that her discipline was improving, contrary to the facts.

Madeline properly behaved when she was with Karen and always told her that school was going fine. The school was unable to contact her; they did not even make a lot of effort as they thought she was out of those who were never going to make it out of school.

Her actions were getting more intense by the day. One day she crossed the line. Along with the brats she stayed with, they planned to prank a teacher, and Madeline was encouraged by the group to lead the activities. Taking it as an honor and not knowing what the consequences could be, she embraced the role and was even responsible for making the entire plan.

She asked one of her friends to get her some glue. The next day, prior to the teacher entering the class, she walked up to the teacher's chair and applied glue on it. She settled down in class, waiting for the teacher, and hoping to please her friends by pulling out the prank. As soon as the teacher entered, she placed her bag on the desk, greeted the students, and sat on the chair. The moment she sat down, Madeline started smiling. She did not like the teacher and was attending her class after quite a few days. The teacher, too, was surprised to see Madeline in class after so many days but did not ask her why she had missed so many classes, mainly because she did not want to get engaged with someone as outspoken as Madeline was. When her teacher got bothered with her continually smiling, she enquired what the reason was. Madeline replied that nothing was wrong but did not stop smiling.

The teacher was agitated but preferred not to display her emotions of anger. She ignored Madeline and continued with the class. She sat on her chair the entire period. After the bell rang, she tried to stand up, but she was unable to move. Not in any part of her mind had she imagined that there was something wrong with the chair but instead tried harder, wondering if something wrong had happened to her.

She pushed herself off the table, and the force tore apart her skirt right from behind. She was embarrassed. The entire class stood there, staring at what had happened, and the brats even started to laugh. By the time the teacher got aware of the situation, Madeline had already left. She had figured out straight away that Madeline had a part to play in it. The constant smiling and being the only student leaving the class, she was confident that Madeline had something to do with it.

The next day when she got to school, she was immediately called over to the principal's office. When she got there, she already saw her friends standing there. It wasn't hard to figure out why they were there. The teacher, whom they had pranked, was also present, and when she asked if she had anything to do with the incident, Madeline denied. The next thing said to her was very surprising. All her friends had confessed that Madeline was responsible and that they had advised her not to prank the teacher, but she refused.

Madeline was in a state of shock. She did everything to please her friends and all of them, without any hesitation, held her responsible. Madeline was speechless. She was made to sit in the office the entire day. She wondered what action they were going to take against her, and she thought she would get away with it just like she did with everything else.

Karen came to pick her up and made her way to the principal's office. When she got there, she saw Madeline sitting in one corner expressionless. She asked Madeline if everything was alright to which Madeline showed no reaction. The principal then started speaking about

Madeline's story. He began with her declining performance in academics. He then moved on to how her behavior was deteriorating by the day, and then she was told about the prank. Karen couldn't believe what she was hearing. She had worked her to groom Madeline and had taught her all the etiquettes. She was in disbelief. She asked the principal if he was sure that he was talking about the Madeline sitting right in front of him, and not some other girl named her. Tears were running down her cheeks, and she apologized to the principal for all the inconvenience caused by her daughter.

The apology was never going to be enough. The principal expelled Madeline from school, and Karen was very disappointed. She requested the principal to reconsider the expulsion decision and asked to look for alternative solutions. The principal denied any reconsideration, and it was the last day for Madeline at the school. The demon was successful in causing trouble for Madeline through the bunch of kids who were under his influence, and in the absence of the Guardian's help, she was to suffer only.

Chapter 4
Sunflowers

Time was doing its trick as it did for everyone else. Madeline was growing both physically and mentally. Time off from school had made her re-think about all the decisions she had made. Those decisions were not crucial but rather idiotic. She was so involved with the bunch of brats that she had forgotten the values she had absorbed from Karen.

The magic wand of time had made her taller, and her cognitive functionality had improved. She was always smart, and if it was not for the bad influence, she wouldn't have ever been rusticated. Karen was quite concerned about what had happened at school. She was angry with what Madeline did.

Karen tried to understand the reason behind her behavior but was unable to create any understanding. Karen was drowning in self-doubt. She was blaming herself for Madeline's action as she was unaware of how special Madeline was. Karen had no idea that both good and evil powers were battling to have Madeline on their side. For her,

Madeline was just a normal child, who had become disobedient and mischievous, which definitely was not the case. What made Karen even more confused was to see her daughter act normally at home. She was expecting Madeline to misbehave or do something that would cause displeasure to Karen, but there was nothing that had changed about her. Karen even started to ignore Madeline a great deal. She practiced ignorance to make Madeline realize that she was not happy with what she had done. Madeline, on the other hand, knew her mother was not pleased with what she had done.

By then, Madeline was not happy with her actions herself. Life lessons learned through experiences are few and far between. No matter how good is the guidance and how easy to understand are the consequences, if Madeline hadn't experienced all of it herself, she probably wouldn't have ever learned. Madeline had become a different person, particularly after the last incident, which was perhaps the first time she felt embarrassed. She had never seen Karen cry, and she is the reason her tears had made her sad. Madeline had learned quite a bit after being expelled. She understood what expectations are and what happens when a person does not value those expectations. She also learned the true meaning of friendship and connections. When she saw how worried Karen was for her because of how careless her newly made friends were, she was able to distinguish between honest and fake emotions. She learned to respect the emotions of people associated with her and regretted the discomfort she had caused to her teachers. Realization is good, but too much awareness tampers the confidence and self-esteem of a person. Madeline was in this phase of over-realization.

Out of all the things, Madeline was confident that she was not going to be surrounded by people who appeared as friends but weren't. She had become very conscious. Karen knew that if Madeline stayed home for long, it would sabotage her self-confidence to an even higher degree than it already had. Karen had shortlisted a few schools and wanted to get her in a school that focused on discipline. Karen had developed a theory that since Madeline spent most of her time with Karen and nobody else, she never learned how to behave with other people.

Karen thought it gave her a sense of freedom, which is why Madeline got herself into a state of carelessness where all she was concerned about was having fun. Had she known that Madeline was the chosen one and had supernatural threats, she would have discarded the theory right away. Finally, Karen found a suitable school for her daughter. Madeline was to rejoin school at the primary level, and she was excited to get back to school. She probably wouldn't have been thrilled if it was the same school, but since it was a fresh start, Madeline was looking forward to it.

The new school was not as big as the previous as well as it had fewer students in comparison. The structure of the school was very artistic. It was beautifully constructed and was an inspirational place for creative people. Madeline loved the new location and was excited to start school again. Madeline was a different girl in the new school. She was more conscious and did not trust anybody. She had lost faith in friendships and had learned that there was no one she could trust. Her experience at the previous school was very embarrassing, due to which she was motivated to ensure that she did not make the same mistakes she had made in her earlier school.

Karen was noticing that Madeline was acting differently. Madeline used to be a bubbly girl full of energy, who would always be seeking adventures. But with time comes change, and time passed. Karen at first thought that her daughter was growing up and had become more mature. She also did not want to encourage her to become the same Madeline she was at the previous school. However, gradually, she realized that it wasn't maturity, but rather, Madeline had become a different person.

She lacked confidence and did not enjoy anyone's company aside from Karen's. At first, Karen pretended if the way Madeline had started behaving was natural and if that was how she was supposed to act. Mainly because all Karen had in mind was to ensure that Madeline managed to continue school.

Karen knew that Madeline was a bright kid and that her past results did not reflect her daughter's potential. She hoped that after a few days at school, Madeline would adjust to the environment, and would get back to who she was. But when she realized that there was nothing that was changing with Madeline, her concerns started growing stronger. Karen saw that her daughter remained silent most of the time and only responded when she was asked to; otherwise, she did not participate in any discussion or even in any activity for that matter. As a mother, it was Karen's responsibility to ensure that her daughter was confident and was not suffering from any stress. She decided to talk to her daughter and motivate her, hoping that it would pull her daughter out of the darkness she was sinking in. One day, Karen waited for Madeline to return from school. Karen had recently moved to a new house, which was closer to Madeline's new school.

The house was not as big as the previous one. There were only two rooms with attached bathrooms and a kitchen. The kitchen did not have an entrance and shared space with the lounge. The lounge only had one couch where Karen would sit and read. Madeline mostly stayed in her room. When Madeline returned from school, she found Karen sitting on the couch. Karen asked Madeline to join her as soon as she entered the room.

"How was school?" Karen asked, padding the empty space on the couch right next to her, indicating Madeline to join her there.

"It was good, mama," Madeline replied, walking toward the couch sitting beside her mother.

"I'll tell you a story, child," Karen continued caressing her daughter's hair and pulling her head to her shoulder. Madeline placed her head on her right shoulder and started listening.

"Once there was a princess who lived in England," Madeline had all her attention centered towards the story. *"She was stunning and had long brown hair, just as yours,"* Madeline looked at her mother and smiled.

"She was not a smart student, and her mother, the queen, was very unhappy about it. The princess wanted to make her mother happy and started working hard to improve her results. After some time, the queen noticed that her daughter was getting better results. The queen became extremely happy by her daughter's performance and hosted a royal dinner. Everybody in the palace was very happy. The royal dinner had all sorts of fruits and cuisine. And everyone was having a great time. But the queen noticed that out of all the people, the only person who did not seem happy was the princess."

Madeline interrupted, *"Why wasn't the princess happy?"*

"The queen did not know, nobody did."

"Then what did the queen do?" Madeline asked out of curiosity.

"I wish I knew, my child, because my princess here does not seem happy either. I'm no queen, baby, but you here are a princess. Mommy's princess," Karen said, kissing Madeline's forehead.

Madeline smiled back at her mother and kept resting her head on her shoulder. It was after quite some time that Karen had seen her daughter smiling. She only hoped that Madeline got over whatever happened at the previous school and moved on, which is why Karen never spoke to her again about anything that happened there.

The Guardian's health had improved, and it was time for her to return. The Guardian had to see if Madeline was ready and rightly the chosen one. She knew that her absence would have caused Madeline a lot of trouble, and she was there to see the impact of those troubles. The Guardian was aging, and it couldn't have delayed the transfer of power any further. The powers transfer in a matter of hours or days; the Guardian started the power transferring process. If the powers transfer all of a sudden, Madeline could have misused them, as Madeline herself was growing as a person.

When the Guardian returned, she evaluated Madeline and realized that Madeline, the chosen one, was a different person. She had become more mature and responsible, and she was ready to have the first taste of her powers. However, Madeline did not know that she had the Guardian overlooking her and that she was to get supernatural powers. The Guardian decided to gift Madeline powers that uplifted her spirits. Madeline had not only grown mature but had also become a dark person. Nothing gave her happiness, and there was nothing that got her excited. The Guardian also observed Karen's concerns for her daughter and passed on the gift to Madeline.

At school, the only activity that Madeline enjoyed was painting. Being a young child, she was not good at it. The gift passed on to her by the Guardian had added energy in her life; nonetheless, she had no idea as to how she was going to release or utilize that energy. One day at school, she was sitting alone at lunchtime like she always did and started painting. This was not the first time she was painting, but on this occasion, it was different. All she had to do was place her hand on the canvas, and the magic happened itself. Her paintings were amazing. She painted beautiful sceneries of places she had never visited. The staff of the school was surprised to see a young girl paint so flawlessly. Her paintings appeared as though they were painted by a professional painter. Her teacher even gifted her a canvas, which she was allowed to carry home. When Madeline took the paintings home, Karen was stunned to see them. Karen did not believe that all these paintings were made by Madeline. She did not say that to her but grew concerned that her daughter was involved in something indecent. She thought so because she assumed that Madeline had started lying, which was not the case.

The same day, Madeline started painting on the canvas at home. Karen saw her painting of a tuxedo cat and was amazed at how her daughter was so indulged in painting that she did not really pay attention to anything around her. Karen pondered for a split second the possibility that the cat was the same one as the night she found Madeline. It was almost as if Merlin purred from the vibrant painting. Like an artist, all her attention was focused on the colors and canvas, and whatever she made would be immaculately perfect. Karen was relieved that her daughter was not lying to her, and was really glad to see progress in Madeline's attitude.

Karen always knew that Madeline was a unique child. From a very young age, she noticed Madeline was different from the other children. She had started speaking way earlier than average toddlers did, and this was the case with Madeline walking. Karen somewhat closed her eyes to everything that Madeline did in an exceptional manner, mainly because she was unable to reason to any of it. Karen often wondered if Madeline's parents were extraordinary people since she had never met them, all she could do was assume and predict.

Madeline had started to enjoy painting, but her mood had not changed much. She was still the same girl sinking into darkness. The Guardian put a picture of a sunflower in her mind for Madeline to paint. Madeline woke up in the middle of the night and went to the lounge. There she placed the canvas on the floor right in front of the couch and started painting. She started painting a sunflower. As she finished painting, it was hard to tell if the sunflower was painted on the canvas or if it was a real sunflower lying on top of it. Madeline loved the painting herself, and the bright yellow color of the sunflower added color to her life. She felt a lot better as if there was some weight on her soul that was removed after the painting was completed. She stared at the painting for over thirty minutes, and every minute made her feel better. After a while, she went back to bed and fell asleep.

When Karen woke up the next day, she was surprised to see the luminous painting lying in the lounge. Karen was sure that there was no painting lying in the room when she went to bed, which was after Madeline had slept. She went to see Madeline if she was awake. Madeline seemed to be in a deep sleep. Karen ignored her thoughts and made herself believe that the painting was lying there since last night. She returned to the kitchen to prepare breakfast for Madeline, ignoring her feelings.

When Madeline woke up and went into the kitchen, Karen asked her why the painting was lying in the lounge in front of the couch. Madeline pretended that she was unaware when she placed it there. She remembered that she had woken up in the middle of the night and painted; however, she did not tell Karen about it because she did not want to get her mother worried. Karen noticed that Madeline seemed to act differently. She looked like the excited little girl she used to be, or in fact, even happier.

The Guardian had succeeded in her mission. The evil power had an insight into everything that was happening, and his concerns were only increasing. He knew that if things continued this way, soon, the Guardian would be successful in transferring the powers to Madeline. He also knew that if he did not revise his plan for influencing Madeline negatively, otherwise he might fail to stop her from becoming the next Guardian. It was his chance of putting an end to any competition in the future, but the evil was not sure how he was to do it.

Chapter 5
Mystery Makes Mess

Madeline had now turned 14 years old. As she was growing, so were her skills over the canvas. Her canvas was a true reflection of how she felt. Whenever she felt happy, she used bright colors to illustrate something beautiful and lively. Conversely, when she felt low, she would use dark colors and carve images of the night.

Karen noticed how her interest in painting was only increasing over time. She was not at all concerned about it. She was, in fact, glad that her daughter was engulfed in a healthy activity. Her fear that Madeline's behavior would not change much when compared to the terrible one she had in her previous school was gradually fading. She always thought Madeline was special and how she used the colors over the canvas only cemented her faith in Madeline being unique.

The Guardian had a close eye on Madeline and had groomed Madeline in a way that enabled her to live away from danger. The guardian was like a shadow to Madeline.

It stayed with her without interfering. This was the final phase, which confirmed that Madeline was rightly the chosen one. In this phase, the Guardian had to evaluate Madeline's personality and determine whether Madeline's character was suitable to behold the powers or not. Madeline had successfully passed the final stage, and she became tender and considerate of others. She respected her mother and stopped doing anything that made her feel unhappy and disappointed.

She had found an activity that allowed her to think beyond her visual capacity and explore unknown dimensions. The colors gave her hope and served as a motivation to not hold back from imagination, but count on it. Karen believed it was the new school, which was responsible for turning around Madeline's personality. To Madeline, it was never really in her control. It was a battle between the evil power and the Guardian, and Madeline's actions reflected which one of the two was having the upper hand.

The new school and a different environment had worked in Madeline's favor. Her creative skills had helped her gain a decent reputation, unlike how things were at her previous school. Madeline's teachers were satisfied with Madeline's performance, and most of them admired how talented the young girl was. This is why Madeline enjoyed time at school, and with the canvas at home, she never felt like going out or doing anything else. Since she preferred to stay at home more often than not, it had become even more difficult for the evil powers to influence Madeline with any negativity. The Guardian decided that the time had come to show signs to Madeline – even reveal to her the powers and the responsibilities which were about to be transferred to her.

She decided to use her powers and meet Madeline in the dream. That night, Madeline finished her last art piece before going to bed, as she always did, and fell asleep as soon she hit the bed. It was a kind of sleep she had never fallen in before. She felt her hair caressed by the wind, while her blanket massaged her feet. It was all because of the Guardian because to have Madeline's complete attention, she had to ensure that Madeline was in a deep sleep.

The Guardian met Madeline in her dream. Madeline felt as if she were awake, which she actually was not. In her dream, she was following a path that was paved from between a river. Birds were chirping, and purple colored flowers were blooming on both sides. It was exactly like the painting she had drawn prior to sleeping. She kept on walking through the path, waiting to reach the other end in her dream, eagerly curious to figure out what was waiting for her on the other side. When she reached the other end, there was nothing. All she could see was a bright light. The light seemed to have a voice – the voice of the guardian. *"Welcome, my child,"* the Guardian addressed Madeline, who looked around confused, trying to figure out where the voice was emanating from. Soon, she realized that the voice was meant to come from a place she could not witness. She did not say a word.

Karen coincidentally had a dream that Madeline was not lying on her bed. She woke up right away and rushed to check in on to Madeline. When she got there, she saw Madeline fast asleep, and Karen, relieved, went back to her bed. She did not know that Madeline was, in fact, far away mentally on her visit to the Guardian.

The Guardian told Madeline that she was the protector and had grown old. Madeline was told that she was the chosen one. She told her about the new powers and responsibilities bestowed upon her. However, for the transfer to be complete, she would have to give up something that was very close to her heart. She was also told that she had to give it to someone who was more in need of it than she was. Since Madeline was having the conversation in her dream, she could not have asked the Guardian to be more specific. As soon as the Guardian finished, the light disappeared, and it all turned pitch black. Madeline opened her eyes, and she realized she was lying in her room. She immediately started thinking about the dream and re-visited the conversation by recalling its vivid details. Madeline had understood that she was the chosen one, but she did not know what for. All she could do was figure out what she had to give up to have another visit by the Guardian, where the rest of the truth was to unfold. Feeling confused, Madeline forced herself back to sleep.

The following morning, Madeline woke up thinking about everything important to her. The first thing that came to her mind was Karen. Karen was significant to Madeline, and her heart was very close to her mother. But she definitely needed Karen more than anyone else did. However, the last part of the Guardian's statement confirmed that it was not referring to Karen. Clueless to how the puzzle was supposed to be solved, Madeline hoped that she would figure it out soon. A couple of days had passed, and yet Madeline had no clue about what the Guardian was talking about. Madeline kept on thinking about it, whether she was at school or at home, but there was nothing that fitted the description of the details provided by the Guardian. She even doubted that the Guardian was talking about her canvas.

The painting was not just her habit, but it was an activity she had fallen in love with. Madeline started searching for somebody who needed the canvas more than her but failed to come across anybody who needed it. She did happen to meet a boy who liked painting. However, he was not as passionate about the canvas as Madeline. Also, the boy had his own canvas, which illuminated the point that he was in need of it more than Madeline was.

A whole week had passed by, but Madeline was yet to identify the thing she had to sacrifice. Lying in her bed, thinking about everything that was in her possession, she started thinking that it was a dream and had nothing to do with reality. She had thought it over hundreds of times and then came to the conclusion that there was nothing in her possession to give, which the Guardian demanded of her.

When she rolled over from her right side to her left, she noticed the stuffed toy lying right beside her. At that moment, she realized what she had to give up. The Guardian, for her part, was referring to the stuffed toys she had since her childhood. The stuffed toys were always with Madeline, and she still slept next to them. She did not know why she had to get rid of them, but Madeline, having a heart of a giver, did not think twice before putting them away. Unfortunately, the intention to put them away was not sufficient. She had to figure out who needed them more than she did. The stuffed toys always made her feel comfortable, and since her childhood, she had never slept in their absence.

Madeline started hunting for the right owner for her stuffed toys, which was ideally someone who needed them more than Madeline did. This meant she needed to find somebody who either had lost his or her parents or did not have anything to play with. There was nobody of such kind that Madeline knew. Obviously, it was not something an elder would require, so Madeline knew that she had to look for a kid. Once when she was going to the town to attend a festival, Karen had noticed a small town close to their own. Madeline decided to visit and give the stuffed toys to somebody who seemed in need. She set off from her house in the afternoon and reached the town within an hour. The town was barely ten miles away from where Karen and Madeline lived. She crossed one house after another and finally spotted a girl who was trying to catch a butterfly. Madeline did not approach the girl, deciding instead to observe her from afar. She did not know why she was spying on that little girl; she felt as though the little girl was a reflection of her childhood. The girl captured the butterfly and then immediately let go of it in an attempt to recapture it. At first, Madeline was unable to comprehend whether the girl had released the butterfly on purpose, or was it accidentally happening.

After the fifth time, Madeline approached the little girl and asked her what she was doing. The girl told Madeline that she was playing around with the butterfly. When Madeline inquired why she kept on releasing and capturing the butterfly, the girl responded that she had nothing else to play with. Madeline realized that her hunt was over as she had found the right candidate who deserved the stuffed toys more than Madeline did. The evil had eyes on Madeline and was observing every activity of the 14-year-old girl. He was unhappy with how fluidly things were happening and how easily Madeline was approaching the final phase of power transition. Something had to be done that complicated Madeline's livelihood and made things difficult for the Guardian. The devil could not have allowed her to grow into a powerful intellectual. The only way he could stop the transition of power was by weakening Madeline. He influenced the people of the town to fight amongst themselves. This way, he could ensure that Madeline would be surrounded by negative vibes, while Karen would restrict her to stay home while not allowing her to explore. If an immense amount of hate could be perpetuated, then Madeline could even be physically unsafe, which was all the evil power wanted. He wanted Madeline to suffer, and in the process, he did not mind victimizing the entire town.

The residents were divided, blaming each other for the unrest. They did not have any exact reasons for the hatred, and all everyone did was raise their fingers at each other. It would start with an argument, and in a matter of moments, the arguers would turn physical and begin assaulting each other. The fights had become so common that Karen, as expected, did not allow Madeline to go out as she did not want her daughter to get hurt. Madeline even had to paint in her bedroom, away from prying eyes. Initially, she argued and resisted, but when she realized none of her arguments had any impact on Karen's decision, she quit expressing her opinion.

"Mom, if you allow me to go out, I'll fix all of it," Madeline would reason.

"I know you will, honey, but right now, I'd like to see you paint in your room," Karen replied. It was a regular debate between the two of them, all the while things in town were getting worse.

The Guardian, admiring Madeline's intentions, gave her another gift. The second gift which Madeline received was the art of sculpting. Madeline started making sculptures, and the first sculpture she made was of a house. It was a simple yet beautiful sculpture, and Karen, as always, was impressed to discover another talent within her daughter. She encouraged Madeline to continue making sculptures as this was not only going to keep her at home but would also enhance her creativity.

There was a purpose as to why the Guardian had gifted Madeline with the power of making sculptures. Madeline had the spirit of fixing things and had no idea how she was going to succeed in her goal. The Guardian's gift was what she needed, and, unknowingly, the second sculpture she made was a fantastic statue of the leader of the town. Madeline spent two days making that sculpture. Karen knew that Madeline was making sculpting, but did not pay attention to what she was making. When Madeline completed making the statue and showed it to Karen, Karen was blown away.

Madeline insisted Karen take the statue out with her in the market. Madeline believed that by showing the sculpture to the people, she could promote peace. Karen did not agree with the idea because she did not want Madeline to get in trouble. Karen would also not close her eyes to Madeline's talent. Karen would convince herself that her daughter was an ordinary girl despite witnessing some beautiful art, which was extremely difficult to believe was made by a girl in her early teens. Madeline convinced Karen that it was not about her wanting to display her talent and receiving compliments, but that there was something needed to bring people close.

The only way this could be done was by reminding them that they all believed in the leader of the town. Madeline was attempting to divert people's focus on a common agenda, which was to live in peace. The war had already made their living conditions miserable. Karen finally gave up and agreed to carry the statue along with them to place it in the market in order to grab as much attention as they could. Karen and Madeline covered the statue with a cloth and made their way into the market.

They placed it on two blocks and sat beside it, hoping for people to gather around. Karen was nervous, whereas Madeline was confident. The market was stunned to see the statue, and gradually, people started to converge. They all stood around, staring at the statue, realizing that the entire town was in the war crises together. In a matter of a few minutes, almost the whole village had gathered in front of the statue. Madeline had succeeded in her mission, making Karen incredibly proud of her.

The sense of brotherhood that had been dispersed due to the evil powers' influence had been restored. The residents of the town started showing respect toward each other and realized that in times of war, fighting against each other was only going to worsen their situation. Finally, Madeline was able to defeat the mischievous power and moved another step closer to her destiny.

Chapter 6
Cookie Jar

Madeline had gone through two different experiences in school. One of them was as a brat at school, dedicated to behaving as miserably as possible. Her second one was as a decent student and a creative intellectual who had the capacity to interpret reality and make contributions to its improvement. It might have been a little too much for an ordinary 14-year-old, but Madeline was not ordinary.

The peace situation in the town had improved to a great extent, and people had come to terms with living peacefully. Karen's concerns about Madeline's safety were satisfied, and Madeline was allowed to go out more often. Her visits were mostly to the market. Although she had not made many friends, being involved in painting and sculpting suppressed her desire to have any.

Madeline eventually completed school and had passed with decent grades. Karen, who once thought that Madeline might never make it through school, admired her daughter's intelligence. Karen gave Madeline a few coins to buy herself a gift. Madeline hugged her mother and excitedly went to the market to use the money her mother had given her. Madeline loved buying toys from the market. In most of her visits, all she got herself were candies, but on this occasion, she wanted to get herself something different. On her way to the market, she ran into a man who was selling cookie jars. She stopped by his stall for a few moments and then continued walking towards the market.

When she got to the market and started looking for something of her interest, she drifted towards her favorite stuffed toy shop, confidently believing that it was the right place for her to spend the money. All this time, the thought of returning to the man selling cookie jars had not departed. She did not know why she needed a cookie jar. Despite having other options that apparently seemed better, her mind kept on circulating around the cookie jars. Madeline did not resist any further and left the toy shop to return to the first stall she had encountered. It was the stall of cookie jars.

When she got to the stall, she saw that there was no cookie jar on display. Surprised, she questioned the man if all his jars were sold. The man replied, *"Yes, my child, every one of them."* Madeline turned around in disappointment and started walking away from the stall. She had barely taken a few steps when the man drew back Madeline's attention by calling out, *"Girl! Come here."* Madeline swiftly plodded back, expecting good news. *"I knew you would come back. I saved one for you. Cheers!"* he smiled. Madeline thanked the man and bought the cookie jar happily, even though Madeline herself was unaware behind the reason for her happiness.

Eventually, it was time for Madeline to join high school. Karen had motivated Madeline a great deal. Karen gave Madeline some pep talk before she started school, *"You are about to have the best time of your life. You're going to fall in love. You're going to make mistakes. But don't worry about it. Mommy's right here."*

Karen was nervous about making friends because the last time she made friends, they turned out to be everything but her friends. Betrayal and distrust filled her mind. It had become part of her belief system that friendships were not for her. She had never thought about falling in love prior to the time Karen discussed it with her. Even after Madeline started school, she did not make any friends, and neither did her attitude welcome anyone who attempted to communicate with her. She was approached by many peers of her class, but she resisted all of their approaches. Out of all the ones who approached Madeline, Emma was the one who did not stop trying. Emma had a very innocent face, most of which was covered by her wavy dark brown hair. Emma liked how particular Madeline was in making friends. Emma, too, did not like being friends with anyone, and she believed she had found her perfect classmate. Gradually, Madeline grew comfortable and became friends with Emma.

Madeline had started to enjoy high school. She looked forward to her time with Emma and was gradually regaining her positive personality. She had begun looking for exciting activities and ensured that she spent most of her time doing something positive. Emma had more friends than Madeline, but Madeline was undoubtedly her best one. Over time, Emma's friends also became Madeline's acquaintances.

Months passed, and Madeline and Emma's friendship grew stronger. They spent most of their time together at school. Madeline had become quite social, just like Emma, and her friend circle grew. Madeline was growing up and was discovering new dimensions in her life.

Madeline had started liking a boy at school – Mark. She had told Emma about it, and despite Emma's encouragement, she never had the courage to walk up to Mark and confess her feelings. Mark had noticed Madeline staring at him a couple of times, and he figured out that Madeline must have some interest in him. Mark approached her, and they soon became friends. It was only in a matter of days until Mark confessed to Madeline that he really liked her. Madeline, in response, admitted that she liked him, too.

Madeline had fallen in love, and nobody besides Emma knew about her newfound affair. Madeline told Karen about her boyfriend, and Karen was glad that her daughter was growing and experiencing life like any average child. Since an early age, Madeline had surprised her mother continuously by doing something extraordinary. Karen secretly feared if something was wrong with her daughter, which is why whenever Madeline did anything ordinary, it would give Karen some sort of satisfaction. Mark started visiting Madeline more often after school, and they were all happy with their situation.

Emma was the only one not happy with Mark and Madeline's relationship. Emma liked Mark, and she was the first person who encouraged Madeline to talk to Mark. However, little did she think about time differences. After getting into a relationship and falling in love, Madeline spent most of her time with Mark. Emma's share of Madeline's time was significantly reduced, and she was not happy about it.

Emma tried to show her displeasure and started avoiding Madeline. She believed that this way, Madeline would figure out that something was wrong and would speak to her to find out. Madeline was so involved with her art and Mark that she did not pay much attention to Emma's changed attitude. The time Emma and Madeline spent together was reducing day by day. Madeline already had less time to spare for Emma, and Emma's new strategy of avoiding her was only increasing the gap.

Days passed, and nothing changed. Emma decided that it was time for her to confront Madeline and put an end to the awkward situation. Mark and Madeline were sitting together during recess when Emma went over to them and told Madeline that she needed to speak to her about something.

Madeline immediately stood up and walked away with Emma. They went to an empty classroom where Emma complained to Madeline that she was not spending enough time with her. Madeline reasoned that she was occupied with school work. She did not even have time for painting. Emma was referring to the time she spent with Mark. Madeline did not just think about it. Emma explained how she spent most of her time with Mark and that schoolwork did not consume most of her time.

Madeline did not like how Emma was complaining and expected her to react differently. She always knew Emma as someone who was supportive and encouraging. Since the beginning of their friendship, things had been very smooth and swift for both of them. This was the first time they had gotten into an argument. Emma was arrogant and angry because she expected Madeline to accept her mistake and apologize.

However, Madeline preferred reasoning. The argument only grew worse when Emma asked Madeline to make a choice between her and Mark. They were just young high school adults who were quarreling over juvenile matters. Emma was creating mountains out of ant holes. Madeline, on the other hand, was not responding wisely either. They were too young to be dealing with the issue maturely. It was basically two young kids whining over something unimportant and were focusing on disagreeing rather than drawing conclusions. They were on the verge of ending their friendship when suddenly, Madeline started thinking about resolving the matter.

She felt as though a voice was whispering in her ear, advising her to act wisely and not lose her closest friend. Madeline at first tried to ignore the voice, but the voice grew loud enough that she was unable to ignore it. She suddenly interrupted Emma, who was busy trying to convince Madeline that she was at fault. Madeline exclaimed, *"I think you're right. You are the best friend I have. How can I think about losing you?"*

Emma was struck by surprise. She did not have anything else to say. All of a sudden, the argument had ended. Emma hugged Madeline, and as the bell rang, they held hands and walked out of the classroom. Madeline kept on thinking about the voice whispering in her ear. The voice was guiding her to be patient and reasonable. It was telling her that Emma was important and was her true friend. The only satisfying answer she formulated was that the voice in her head was the voice of her sub-conscious and nothing else.. However, the truth is that it was of the Guardian. It was trying to protect Madeline from making a mistake, a mistake that would have cost Madeline her friendship. This was not the first time the Guardian had influenced her to make the right decision, but earlier, she had noticed something about the whispering voice. She never had the slightest clue about the supernatural power's guidance. Even then, she was not sure that it was an external entity that was helping her out in making the right decisions. Regardless, doubts had entered her mind.

Madeline had not used the cookie jar she had brought from the man selling it at the stall. One day when she returned from school, she found Karen baking cookies. Madeline loved the cookies Karen baked. When Madeline had the first bite of the cookie, it reminded her of the cookie jar she had recently brought under her possession. She went straight to her room, picked the cookie jar that was lying on the dressing table, and gave it to Karen – asking her to fill it up with cookies. Karen smiled at Madeline and filled the jar with cookies.

Madeline did not know what was special about the cookie jar. The Guardian had designed the cookie jar for Madeline, and it had the potential to do a lot more than just store cookies. It was the Guardian who had convinced Madeline to exit the stuffed toys shop and buy herself a cookie jar. Unbeknownst to Madeline, she was not buying a cookie jar, but something far more valuable.

The cookie jar was elegant, and Madeline loved to carry it wherever she went. Once, she came across a sick man. Madeline offered him a cookie, telling him that it would improve his health. Madeline said that because she saw how the man was depressed and wanted to lift his mood. The man smiled and ate the cookie.

The cookie jar was a tool that the Guardian had given to Madeline. Each day, a person eating from the jar would benefit from it – like the man who recovered his health after having a cookie. When Madeline found out about how people eating cookies out of the cookie jar were benefitting from it, she understood that she was guided by an invisible hand that always guided her in the right direction. So was the case with the people who had the cookies from her cookie jar.

Every day a person was guided in the right direction as every day, Madeline gave someone a cookie out of it. Madeline only offered one person a cookie every day. She also made sure the person she was offering the cookie to was in dire need of help or guidance. Madeline actively looked for the most depressed person. Even though it was hard to gauge the intensity of neediness, in the back of her mind, she was confident because she knew the Guardian was there to help her through it.

Once she saw a man sitting outside a pharmacy, weeping. Madeline asked him what was wrong. Madeline had already given a cookie from the jar the same day to an old woman who she thought had excessive anger issues. Madeline believed that by having a cookie, the old woman would become a calm lady.

However, when she came across this man, she decided to inquire what was wrong. The man only told her that he was not feeling well and needed money to buy his medications. Madeline did not have any money in her pocket as she had already given away the day's cookie. She asked the man to meet her in the same place the next day. The man was in desperate need of help and was there as promised. He was expecting to be paid as all he needed was money. When Madeline went to him and offered him the cookie, the man got angry but did not show his anger as he did not want to scare the young girl off. He controlled his anger and took a deep breath. Then, he ate the cookie in one go. He was lucky because if he had not had the cookie, things would have been much worse for him.

The man from the pharmacy store was to go to a bank as he was not expecting Madeline to bring a lot of money with her and definitely did not think she would come to him empty-handed. He did not know how the cookie could ease his problems. The man could not have afforded to have his application rejected by the bank for the loan.

He had made up his mind that he was going to create a story about having a business idea and would apply for a business loan instead of a personal loan. It was a life and death situation. The cookie did not just heal people medically but also had a spiritual impact. It guided them to do the right thing, like being honest and fair. The man did not lie when filing his application. He did not feel like being dishonest. This is what the cookie from the jar did. It made people do the right thing. Soon, Madeline realized that she could use the cookie jar even more effectively by targeting the essential people of the town. She gave it to corrupt police officers and people associated with the civil services. She also gave it to the Mayor of the town. Slowly but surely, the town was becoming an ideal place to live in.

Madeline even offered the cookies to the thieves and muggers of town. Just as the cookies were effective for everyone else, so were they for the thieves. Corruption significantly reduced in the town, and the crime rate had fallen down extraordinarily. The town became a peaceful place as everyone made the right decisions and had no evil intentions, and it was all because of Madeline and her cookie jar.

Chapter 7
Where is Home?

Madeline had turned the town into a very peaceful place. The war had continued for quite long, and people had become used to living in circumstances that were not peaceful. People had forgotten what living in peace was like. The war had made them impatient and paranoid. Almost every town affected by the war fell into unrest – one where people had become wholly intolerant and frustrated.

The only town that lived in peace was the town where Madeline lived. If it was not for Madeline, the conditions of her town would not have been any different when compared to the other villages surrounding it. The statue Madeline had crafted had allowed people to re-think and realize what the war was about and what was lost in the process. Madeline helped them revisit their ideology, allowing them to understand that they were the ones suffering, and the only way they could make it through the fierce war was unity.

The cookie jar Madeline received from the Guardian had helped her immensely with making the town a peaceful place. Their community was no different than the adjacent towns in terms of hatred and turmoil. However, through Madeline's efforts and the Guardian's assistance, the town was now in peace. The evil power was astounded to see the revolution initiated by the little girl. The evil believed that the little girl was incapable and would not be able to make a difference, even with the help of the Guardian. It was unaware that Madeline was a girl with a very pure heart, and that through the Guardian's gifts, she could make a phenomenal difference.

Madeline was delighted with her life. Her academic performance in school was terrific, and she was doing wonders on the canvas. She liked everything about her school, and Karen was satisfied with how her daughter's life was proceeding. Also, Madeline's new relationship had made things easier for her. From being someone who did not participate in many activities, Madeline had now become someone who enjoyed taking part in everything. Emma, Madeline, and Mark spent most of their time together at school, and their friendship was growing stronger by the minute. Madeline had already become an inspiration for the people of the town and was content with life. Life has a pattern of ups and downs. Whenever there is linearity in the equation of life, one must expect an inevitable rise or fall. Things never remain pleasant or miserable for a very long period. The beauty of life lay in adventure, struggle, and surprises, and not all of these are pleasing. One day, when Madeline was walking home from school, she suddenly had a weird feeling, as if something was not right. She wished that it was nothing but a false signal. Upon reaching home, she realized that Karen was not home.

Karen would always be home to welcome Madeline when she got back from school. It was the first time Karen was not there. Madeline, already sensing that something was not right, eagerly watched the door hoping Karen would walk in any moment. After an hour passed, Madeline realized that she could not sit and wait for her mother to return. She had to do something, and the least she could do was look for her in the market or neighborhood. Madeline was growing anxious as the clock was ticking. Finally, when the sky was changing colors, and it was getting dark, Madeline decided to leave her house and search for her mother. Madeline set off for the market. She had barely walked a few yards when she spotted something lying further in the distance. She carefully walked close to it, not knowing what it was. She had little fear in her heart as it did seem like a person and not an object. As soon as she got close, she rushed towards it as she realized it was Karen.

Madeline had tears in her eyes as she ran towards her mother, calling her out and demanding a response. Karen was lying on the ground, motionless. Madeline was not strong enough to lift her mother. She looked for help, but since the path to the market was not a crowded one, she was unable to find anyone who could.

Madeline hopelessly started crying as she thought her mother had died. She sat right next to her mother, paced her head on her lap, and kept on weeping. Suddenly, she was confronted by a man who claimed to be passing by. The man, without asking or saying a thing, lifted Karen, and they rushed to the doctor. There was not much the man needed to ask as he could clearly see why the young girl was crying.

When they reached the clinic, which was run by a local in the town, the man-in-charge immediately took Karen into a room and asked Madeline to wait outside. The man who had brought Karen to the hospital with Madeline had disappeared. Madeline did not know who he was, and neither did she know where he had gone. Little did Madeline know, the man was sent by the Guardian.

After a couple of hours, the doctor stepped out of the room. Madeline rushed to him, crying out, *"Is my mother fine?"*

"For now," the doctor answered, sitting on the vacant chair placed in the waiting hall. He tapped the seat of the second chair, inviting Madeline to sit beside him. Madeline sat there, and after staring for a second with her expressions clearly demonstrating disbelief and lack of comprehension, she asked, *"What do you mean?"*

The doctor explained to her that her mother had a tumor in her brain. He told Madeline that there was not much they could do and that Karen was not to live for long. Madeline felt numb. She felt as though her heart had stopped beating. The doctor rubbed Madeline's back, trying to comfort her as tears flooded out of her eyes. Madeline was very close to her mother.

She was the only parent she had, and there was no way she could lose her. The doctor told Madeline that she could take her mother back home the next morning. He handed over a prescription to her and told Madeline that she had to ensure her mother took the medicines on time. When Madeline asked for the bill to be paid to get her mother discharged, the doctor smiled and said, *"Save it for the medicines. They are not going to be cheap."* Madeline spent the night at the clinic with her mother. The war had destroyed hospitals, and people were only left with clinics for treatment. She spent the entire night sitting on a chair placed right next to her mother's bed. She did not sleep for a second and had cried so much the whole night that her eyes had turned dark red.

The following morning, Karen woke up when the drug lost its effect. She asked Madeline what had happened, and Madeline gently explained to her that she had tripped. She did not mention that the doctor had said that her mother would not live for long, nor had Madeline accepted the diagnosis of the doctor. She refused to believe that her mother was not going to live for long. Before discharging Karen, the doctor told her about her condition, and Karen tolerated the news. Madeline admired how firmly and calmly her mother had taken the news. The only thing Karen worried about was Madeline, and all she cared about was to make sure that her daughter managed it after her death. After all, there was not anything Karen could have done to change the reality.

Karen needed extra care, and the drugs were making her weak. Also, the medicines were expensive, and Karen was not in a position to work. Madeline also realized that her mother was sick and could not work. She decided to get a job in order to pay for the medications. Madeline was very grateful to the doctor for not charging them with any money.

After returning home from the clinic, Madeline had decided that she was not going to attend school and start working instead. She immediately went to Emma's house, who lived close by. She told her what had happened to Karen and that she was not going to be attending school. She also asked Emma to inform Mark.

Madeline started searching for jobs and finally got one at a farm close by. Everyone in the town knew who Madeline was, especially after the sculpture she had created that got the people of the town together. The owner of the farm was very nice to Madeline and offered her a job right away. However, Karen wanted Madeline to attend school and succeed in life. She argued that her daughter should continue school, but Madeline talked her out. Madeline said she would join back school once Karen regained her excellent health, but Karen knew it was never to happen as the doctors had already told her likewise.

Madeline's job was not easy. It was her first job where she had to work for over nine hours a day. She would get to the farm before the sun rose and would return shortly before the sunset. She never let Karen feel that her daughter had to work extremely hard to pay for her mother's medications. No matter how much she pretended, Karen knew what the reality was. Karen often wept in Madeline's absence because she never wanted her daughter to have a brutal routine.

The evil power was glad about Karen's sickness. Madeline was so involved with the job and in taking care of Karen that she had no time left to paint on the canvas or sculpt statues. More than half of what Madeline earned was consumed by the medical bills, and there was little she was left with to take home. Yet, despite working tirelessly and combating the fears of losing her mother, Madeline always had a wide smile on her face. The only time she did not go to the farm was when Karen had an appointment at the clinic. The owner of the farm was kind enough to even pay her on days when she was absent, which was only once a week on the day of Karen's checkup.

"Did you paint something?" Karen would ask Madeline at regular intervals. Sadly, Madeline would reply, *"I am grown up now; I don't like painting anymore."*

Both Karen and Madeline knew that Madeline enjoyed painting, but the job of the farm was very exhaustive, and by the time Madeline reached home, she had no energy left to play with colors and canvases. The Guardian had a close eye on Madeline. The Guardian admired the efforts of the young girl and decided to support Madeline – even though it never directly gave Madeline a gift, or help for that matter.

Madeline always made herself out as someone deserving, and in case of Karen's sickness, it was no different. Days passed by, and nothing changed. Madeline managed to purchase the medicines routinely through her job, but Karen's condition kept on deteriorating. Mark visited Madeline regularly, but Madeline would be so occupied with the job and taking care of her mother that she did not have a lot of time to offer. Mark understood Madeline's situation and gradually started delaying his visits. He knew that Madeline was already under a lot of physical and mental stress, so he did not want to do anything that added to her misery. Emma also regularly visited Madeline. Every day after school, Emma would stop by at Karen's, spend time with her, and take care of her while Madeline would be at work. Emma would spend little time with Madeline on her return from work and would then leave.

The economic situation of the entire region was unstable due to the war. Most people living in the town had to work day and night to make both ends meet. Mark and Emma's family were also among the majority of the people who had both their parents working to make a living. Despite wanting to help Madeline, there was not much they could do.

Karen would talk to Emma about how sorry she was to have her daughter working hard to take care of her. Emma would tell her that everything would be fine, as that is what Emma would have done as well. Emma never told Madeline that her mother was upset that Madeline had to work because of her because she, too, did not want Madeline to take on more stress than she already had.

The Guardian decided to bless Madeline with the power of healing. It knew that the long working hours were draining out Madeline, and she was growing weak. Madeline had stopped engaging in any activity which gave her pleasure, but only because she did not have the time and energy to get involved in it. The Guardian knew it had to do something to ease Madeline's life, and the only way that could be done was by improving Karen's health.

The Guardian had to help Madeline in a way that not only helped improve her situation temporarily but also had long-term effects. The Guardian chose to give Madeline the power of healing as, through the power of healing, it would not only make it easier for Madeline to save her mother but would also allow her to help other people around her.

One day, when Madeline was deep in her sleep, she had a dream. In the dream, she was running along the riverside, smiling at people who were crossing by. She then sat on a stone chair, holding an empty glass in her hand. While sitting on the chair, she immersed the empty glass in the river and gave it to anyone who came walking to her. Whoever drank the water smiled at her, kissed her on the forehead, and returned the empty glass of water back to her. It happened continuously – one person after another just kept on coming to her until suddenly she woke up in the middle of the night. Madeline did not know what the dream was about, but since it was not the first time she had had such a bizarre dream, she knew it had a message embedded in it. The next day, Madeline pondered over her dream and tried to interpret its meaning. While walking back home, she spotted a young boy sitting on the corner of the street. The boy seemed exhausted. Madeline walked up to him and asked if everything was alright.

The boy said he was not feeling well and needed some water. Madeline had a water bottle which she took with her to work. She opened it up and offered the boy to have a sip. As soon as the boy drank from the bottle, he seemed fresh. He smiled at Madeline, kissed her on the forehead, and ran away. It seemed as though he was completely healthy and was never exhausted. Madeline recognized the new gift she had received – *"the gift of healing."*

Chapter 8
Deep Hearts

Madeline had become a completely different person after realizing that she was not an ordinary girl, but someone special. She was growing to an age where she could reciprocate the realities of life and distinguish between natural and superficial attributes. The Guardian had trained Madeline in a way that had allowed her to think beyond her sight. She visualized her short journey of life in a flashback and was now moving toward the end of her teen years – she was indeed excited.

Out of all the gifts she had received from the Guardian, *"the gift of healing"* was the one she was the most in need of as Karen's health was only getting worse day by day. This was not the first power Madeline was bestowed upon by the Guardian. Her skill over the canvas and her talent of sculpting were all gifts she had received from the Guardian, but the gifts she had received prior to the power of healing were all sorts of abilities that were difficult for Madeline to comprehend as gifts. The gift of healing was unique. Also, considering her mother's deteriorating health, Madeline was in dire need of it. It was the first time Madeline began realizing that the Guardian was real and not just a figure created by her imagination. Although she had cured the little boy, she was yet not confident whether it was she who had healed him or was it just a coincidence. Karen had become weak. The doctors were not sure how long she was to live, and they had told Madeline as much. Madeline did not have the time to think over her powers or the latest gift she had received from the Guardian. She was mostly occupied with her job at the farm and would spend the remaining time taking care of her mother.

The Guardian had noticed that Madeline had not taken the gift of healing seriously, even in a moment when she needed it the most. It was justified for a couple of reasons. Firstly, she was not sure about receiving any power as she had not encountered a supernatural situation that would have removed all her doubts. Secondly, she was tied up in a tight routine and was only left with little time to introspect.

Madeline had a routine of returning from the farm before dawn. She would get home, check Karen's body temperature, and ensure she had taken all her medications. One day, while exiting the farm, she was stopped by the farm's owner. The farm's owner had some provisions stored and offered them to Madeline. The owner was a very decent man. He knew about Madeline's financial situation, which was why he had also increased her wage. Madeline, at first, refused as she did not want to take any favors from anybody. When the farm's owner insisted, she did not want to be rude and accepted the food. By the time they came to an agreement, it was already getting dark.

Madeline knew that her mother would be worried. She briskly started walking in an attempt to get home quickly. Karen was very overprotective of Madeline. She was always told by Karen to get home before it got dark. Madeline never got late. The only time she did was when she was out with Emma or Mark. While walking back home, Madeline felt amused by the darkness. All the green fields on her path could barely be seen. She could not see anything on either side. Since all Madeline had in mind was Karen, she paid no attention to the apparently dark path ahead.

Suddenly, while walking, she felt as if someone was following her. She turned around to look back a couple of times, but only witnessed darkness. It was the first time she felt afraid. As she took a few more steps, she felt a hand on her shoulder. She did not know whose it was, and out of fear, she did not even turn back to look. She took a pause and started running. Madeline had barely run a couple of yards when she tripped off a stone and fell to the ground. Her knee had bumped into a sharp stone, and it started to bleed. Madeline could see the blood dripping out, but felt no pain. As she sat on the ground, she started looking everywhere to find the person walking along with her. Upon noticing she was alone, she looked down at her bruise and saw it glowing. The light was gradually getting brighter. Madeline stood up, wiped off the dust, and the light slowly began to disappear. Her bruise had gone. It appeared as if she had never been bruised, to begin with.

The light had not disappeared for long. In a matter of seconds, she could see her chest glowing. Standing clueless, Madeline pulled her shirt away from her body and realized that it was not her clothes, but her body that was glowing. Sluggishly, the radius of the glow increased, and Madeline could see it growing. She was in disbelief. Soon, she was covered in light. Her entire body began to glow to such an extent that a person standing right in front of her could not have been able to even look at her. The only thing the person would have witnessed would be light. The aurora of the light expanded, and soon, the entire sky was covered in green light. The light was glowing in a stream as if a shooting star was falling from the sky. However, it was not a shooting star – it was Madeline. Suddenly, the light vanished, and Madeline fell onto the ground. After a few minutes, Madeline gained consciousness. There was no bruise on Madeline's body – not even the scar she had on her right hand that she had gotten from work the same day. She immediately got to her feet and rushed home. Madeline knew that her mother would be very concerned about her. Similarly, Madeline herself was quite worried about Karen. The walk was almost over as she entered into the patch of light from where her home was half a mile distant.

Karen had placed a seat outside the door and was sitting on it, waiting for her daughter to return. She did not have the energy to walk out of her house and look for her daughter. As soon as Karen identified Madeline nearing home, she stood up and called out, *"My child, where have you been?"* Madeline ran towards Karen and gave her a hug.

"Did you take your medications, mom?" Madeline asked. Karen replied, *"Yes. What took you so long? I was so*

worried about you."

Madeline had her reason as on her way back; she had also dropped the parcel given to her by the farm's owner. The last she remembered having it was before tripping on the ground on the dark path. She wanted to share everything that had happened with Karen. However, she was not sure how her mother was to take it. She did not want to put Karen under stress since she was already dealing with a lot due to her deteriorating health. Madeline, instead, made up a story related to work and promised Karen that she would never be late from work again.

Madeline immediately checked her mother's body temperature, which was slightly higher than average. She gave her a pill and lay down next to her. Karen soon fell asleep, but Madeline was consumed by thoughts about what had happened. The glimpse of her knee glowing and healing was all repeatedly circulating in her mind. She knew that she had received a gift.

She started to connect the dots and became certain that she had a part to play in curing the boy of his sickness. The night had passed. Madeline was still in denial. It was difficult for her to believe herself – how on earth was she to convince anyone else. Madeline decided to keep it to herself and not reveal it. She was to test the gift. She had every reason to believe a special power gifted her, and the only thing left to confirm it was by testing it. The next day, Madeline left for the farm on time. Instead of directly walking to the farm, she decided to take a detour and visited a child she knew was sick. Madeline had met the child at the clinic when she had taken her mother there for her weekly checkup. While her mother was taken inside the laboratory for a few tests, Madeline waited outside and met the little boy, who had come along with her mother.

The mother of the boy told Madeline that her son was diagnosed with a severe heart condition, and the doctors believed that he would not be able to enter his teens. The boy was just 9-years-old then. Luckily, Madeline had asked them where they lived, which was not far from her house.

Madeline went to the house and knocked. The mother opened the door and instantly recognized Madeline. She was surprised to have her visit her. Madeline told her she was there to see the boy. Her mother asked if there was any specific reason for which she wanted to see him. Madeline did not want to get the mother curious and told her that she was passing by and decided to stop to say *"Hi."*

The mother invited Madeline inside and took her to the boy's room, where he was lying on his bed. The mother told Madeline in a shaky voice, trying to hold her tears back that the boy was not doing well at all. The mother went outside the room to the kitchen, telling Madeline she was bringing some fresh juice for her. Madeline and the boy were alone in the room. Madeline placed her hand on his chest and closed her eyes. She wanted to help the boy right from the moment she had met him.

She never thought she would be able to do something to improve the boy's health, and the moment she felt capable, the first person she approached to cure was this boy. Madeline opened her eyes and found the boy's chest glowing. There was a light projecting out of Madeline's hand, which was, in turn, absorbed in the boy's chest.

The light eventually faded away, and Madeline removed her hand. As Madeline moved back, the door opened, and the mother entered with a glass of fresh juice. After having the bottle of juice, Madeline requested to take leave. She also inquired about the next appointment at the clinic and promised to visit after it. The boy's mother wished health for

Karen's mother, and the meeting was over. The appointment of the boy was two days later. Madeline had it in mind. She was eagerly waiting for the two days to pass so she could see if she had the capability of healing. The day of the appointment had come, and Madeline went to see the boy and the mother. The mother was more than pleased to see Madeline. She told her how the doctors were surprised to see that the boy had miraculously recovered. Madeline pretended to be surprised herself and acted as if she had no idea how the boy had gotten rid of the disease he had.

Madeline was thrilled. She knew that she had the power of healing, and the thought of healing her mother was overwhelming. She just wanted to get to her mother and practice the healing process on her. The same day she returned home, had dinner with Karen, and lay down next to her. Karen had become very weak and slept for almost half the day, if not more. Madeline placed her hand on her chest and tried to heal Karen. After a few minutes, she realized that it was not working for her mother. She tried it over and over again till the point she felt Karen was being disturbed in her sleep. Left with no choice, Madeline decided to wait for a couple of days and try it again. Three days had passed, but nothing happened when Madeline tried to heal her mother. Madeline thought she had this gift for a short period of time and that she had wasted an opportunity to heal her mother. In order to confirm this theory, she decided to re-test it. Not knowing who she was to help, she went to the clinic and looked for potential patients. She found a man who had breathing problems. She followed the man who lived with his young daughter. Madeline went to the man and told her she could help him with his breathing problem, but only if he promised to keep it to himself.

The man promised that he would keep their meeting a secret. Madeline placed her hand on the man's chest and witnessed the glow radiating from it. The man had started to feel better, but both Madeline and the man could not have known whether he was cured or not unless the doctor performed a few tests. The doctors were again surprised as the man healed. The man was extremely happy and thanked Madeline with gratitude. He said he would always be there if she needed anything. Madeline thanked him for his offer and left. Madeline kept on practicing the treatment on her mother, but not even once did it work.

Madeline had started to become extremely depressed. She decided to speak to Emma about it. She went to Emma's house to see her, where her mother told her that she had gone with her sisters to the neighboring city at her uncle's. Madeline was disappointed that Emma did not inform her before leaving, but did not argue about it with her mother. She then decided to speak to Mark about it. Things between Mark and Madeline had been silent recently. She was not able to spend a lot of time with him, and Mark was not happy about it.

She went over to Mark's place, where she found he was not home. She walked back home, frustrated. When she got home, she found Mark waiting outside. It brought a smile on her face. Mark also spotted Madeline and passed a smile back. When she reached Mark, she hugged him. Mark said he wanted to speak to Madeline about something. Even though Madeline, too, had to talk to Mark about the power of healing, she waited and allowed Mark to speak first.

Mark told her that it was difficult for him to stay in a relationship with her as she was mostly occupied with her own things. He needed some time alone to figure out if he and Madeline could be together. As tears streamed down her cheek, she said Mark could take all the time he wanted. She was angry and already having a tough time. Mark quitting on her made it all worse. It was Madeline's eighteenth birthday the next day, and of all things, she never had expected Mark to leave her on her birthday's eve. Madeline was extremely disappointed. The evil power realized that Madeline was on her low. She was alone and disturbed, which is why it was an ideal time to fill her heart with hate against the Guardian. Madeline started to think about what good the power was for if she could not help her mother.

Madeline started to believe that she was not made to help people. The evil had inserted all these thoughts in her mind. Evil managed to put in so much hate in her heart for the Guardian that she began to think that the Guardian was evil. She believed that the Guardian was giving her powers but with limitations over her authority. She could only heal people the Guardian wanted her to heal. As a result, Madeline decided not to use the powers.

Karen's health kept getting worse. The doctors told Madeline that if Karen's condition kept on deteriorating, she would not survive for long. Madeline and Karen headed back from the clinic, stressed beyond imagination. Madeline did not want to live without her mother, and Karen feared for her daughter facing the world all by herself. As Karen entered through the main entrance, she slipped and fell to the ground. Madeline pulled her close to a sofa lying in the lounge. She somehow managed to get Karen on it and rushed towards the clinic to get a doctor. Shortly, she returned with the doctor, who gave Karen an injection telling Madeline that the night was very critical for her mother. A stroke hit her, and her chances of survival dropped.

The doctor left, and Madeline and Karen were the only ones at home. Karen lay on the couch unconsciously, and Madeline sat right next to her on the floor. Madeline kept on crying unless she felt she needed to give her power another try. The Guardian had put it in her mind. She closed her eyes and put her hand on Karen's chest. A moment later, she witnessed a light coming out of her hand – that same light that had helped her cure the little boy and the man.

The light went away as Karen opened her eyes. Madeline looked at her mother, excitedly. She was glad that her mother was fine. Madeline had started to believe that her mother was completely cured, just like the others. The next day she took her to the clinic where the doctor told her that it was amazing that Karen survived the night, yet she was not entirely out of danger. Madeline did not know why it was not as effective for Karen as it was for the rest. Nevertheless, it helped her mother survive, and she regained hope.

Chapter 9
Is It Real?

Years passed by, and Karen still did not get cured. The expenses of her medications were constantly increasing, and it was getting difficult for Madeline to manage them. Karen was only suffering from the tumor. What had caused her condition to deteriorate more was depression. She felt terrible that her young daughter had to look after her. Karen wanted to make life easy for Madeline by providing her with the best education. Since the moment she had held Madeline for the first time, she had promised herself to take great care of the adorable child. Nonetheless, life had planned things differently for Karen and her daughter.

Madeline began another job. She would work at the farm during the day while she had found a job in a library in the evening. The only reason she had to get another job was to make enough money so that she could afford her mother's medications. Since Madeline was mostly occupied with work, Karen had to spend most of her time alone. The level of depression and anxiety was increasing with each passing day, and her condition was getting worse. Madeline was very concerned about her mother but was unable to spend ample time with Karen. The doctors had warned Madeline that Karen's brain functionality was worsening, and if it continued to stay that way, she might end up falling in a comma. Madeline had tears in her eyes when the news was broken to her, making her feel hopeless and helpless. She did not bother practicing her powers on her mother as she was gradually losing faith in the Guardian and the powers which were bestowed upon her.

Moreover, she could not have risked being late to her job as getting late meant receiving a deducted wage. The medicines were costly, and Madeline valued every cent. The doctors had warned Madeline that if Karen did not get her medications a single day, Karen's nervous system might collapse, taking away her life.

Karen had almost been sick for two years, and every day in the past two years had been long and tiring for Madeline. There was nothing left in the young girl's life besides earning enough to afford her mother's medications. She was struggling to make both ends meet. The situation of the town had gotten worse. The war did not seem to end, and the consequences were disastrous. It had become extremely difficult for people living there to make money. The financial situation of the town was weakening, and the Mayor was unable to formulate any policy that satisfied the town's economic concerns. Since the town was growing poorer day by day, the cost of the medications had significantly increased. The more Madeline earned, the higher the cost of drugs became.

One day, when Madeline returned from work, she found Karen sleeping. Karen had become so weak that she spent most of her time on the bed. Madeline kissed her mother on the forehead like she usually did upon returning home from work. Often, Karen opened up her eyes whenever she felt Madeline kissing her. However, this time, Karen was motionless. Madeline assumed that Karen was in a deep sleep and did not bother disturbing her. Madeline did not even know if her mother had taken her prescriptions, but still did not disturb her mother.

After a couple of hours, when it had gotten late, she decided to wake Karen up. She went to her bed, where Karen was lying and sat right beside her. Madeline had a smile on her face – a smile that only appeared when Madeline looked at her mother. She slowly pressed her arms in order to wake her up, but Karen did not move. By then, Madeline had gotten extremely worried. She shook her a bit harder, yet received no response. Now, Madeline had begun to panic. She cried, *"Wake up mother, I'm here... Please... Moooomm!"* It immediately struck her that she should check if her mother was breathing. She put her finger right in front of her nose and felt her breath. Her mother had to be alive as she was breathing. However, the state of panic had not entirely vanished. It could not have had, as Karen did not move an inch, and neither did she give any reaction to Madeline's attempts to wake her up.

Madeline ran towards the kitchen and grabbed a glass of water. She brought the water close to Karen and dipped her hand in the glass. She then rubbed Karen's face with her wet hand. Even then, she did not get any reaction from her mother. Madeline rushed to the clinic and briefed the doctor on duty about her mother's condition. The doctor grabbed all the equipment he could and hurried with Madeline to her residence. Madeline was constantly crying.

She felt she had lost her mother, and the pain was unbearable. The doctor examined her mother for over twenty minutes. He studied Karen's previous reports and began writing down a prescription. Meanwhile, Madeline kept looking at her mother while briefly glancing over at the doctor. After the doctor finished writing down the prescription, he turned to face Madeline. He held the young girl's hand while caressing her hair with the other. Madeline could intuitively tell something was not right, and her tears dripped down at a quicker pace. The doctor could see Madeline losing control over her emotions and requested her to be patient. He said, *"Child, your mother is alive."* Madeline produced a half-smile, suppressing her tears, which had not stopped dripping. The doctor continued, patting Madeline's head, *"She is in a coma."* The doctor was looking down at his feet as if he had run out of words to console Madeline.

The doctor then handed over a prescription of medications. He added that the medications were expensive – far more costly than the previous ones. Madeline gazed at the doctor in despair. Her expressions had made it evident that she did not know how she was going to afford the drugs listed down on the prescription handed over to her. The doctor realized that Madeline was worried about the medications and that she could not afford them. The doctor picked up the briefcase, which was lying right beside his left leg. He took out a packet and handed it over to Madeline. He told her that all he could do is give her the first box for free. The doctor's eyes had also become watery. He was trying hard to hold his tears, and since everybody in town was struggling with their finances, Madeline knew the doctor was doing the most he could. The doctor left while giving words of courage to Madeline. Madeline, on the other hand, did not know how she was going to buy the next round of medications. She sat the entire night looking at her mother and crying. She sat on the floor, resting her head on her mother's bed. In between tears and prayers, Madeline slept.

The Mayor of the town was failing to provide for its citizens. Most of the people in the town were not paid their salaries, which included policemen, lawyers, doctors, and teachers. The Mayor was worried, but there was nothing he could do to provide for his people. Money was not only needed to deliver paychecks and provide for the citizens, but also for defense purposes. The town had survived the war all because of the Mayor's defense plan. The town had not been directly attacked, but even if it was, a force was prepared to buy enough time for the people to escape. If the town was to suffer through it again, regaining the peace was going to become very challenging – if not impossible. The neighboring town was well aware of the town's situation and figured it was an excellent opportunity to offer help. Help was not offered to improve the town's condition, but to take advantage of the town's situation. Earlier, Madeline had played a vital role in bringing the town together and had eliminated all differences by creating a beautiful sculpture of the leader of the town. This time, the problem at hand was different. The town was in dire need of money, and as most believed, including the Mayor, that an individual could not solve the problem for them at this stage.

The neighboring town offered to buy their local heritage at a reasonable price. The local heritage was the essence of the town that kept the people united. It had a historical association, and the Mayor could not have sold it away unless it was his last choice, which it was. Although he did not want to risk the town's integrity or even peace for that matter, he was left without an option.

The situation of the citizens of the town did not seem to be improving, and the mayor was afraid that he would have to choose between selling the town's heritage and letting it go bankrupt. Madeline had increased her working hours to thirteen. She was aware of the town's situation, but she was so involved in her mother's health that she paid no attention to anything besides work. Even though she was working half of the day, she was still unable to earn enough to buy the next round of medications. She was sleep-deprived, as she would spend most of her time at home, crying and looking at her mother. She would give her all her medications through injections and even fed her that way through a nasogastric tube. She had gotten quite depressed as she was not able to buy the next dose of drugs. Her nights were mostly sleepless and horrific.

She would barely sleep for brief intervals when her body would give up on her, while she would spend the rest of her night cherishing old memories and crying over the present. One night during her sleep, she saw the light again in her dream – the same light that had earlier guided her to solve mysteries and inherent magical powers.

Even if her conscious mind was unwilling to explore and chase her dreams, her sub-conscious mind would make her follow the path that would involuntarily lead her to them. In the dream, she witnessed herself sitting in the middle of an empty room. She was painting on the canvas and was painting at a great pace. What she was painting was astonishing. She was painting a picture in which a girl was creating a sculpture, both things happening simultaneously.

The painting seemed like moving images. As she stroke the brush over the canvas, the sculpture was getting built. She had her arms folded around her head with her face resting on her right cheek. Suddenly, she opened her eyes. In the middle of the night, she began searching for her canvases, which she found were placed below her bed. She placed it in front of her mother's bed and started painting. One painting after another, she kept on doing it until the rays of the sun seeped their way through the glass windows.

Gradually, the entire room was full of light. Madeline stepped back and sat in the vacant corner of the room, facing the window. She was still holding the brush in her hand when she eyed the paintings she had painted. As her mind processed everything that was before her, her eyes shut off, and her mind followed. She woke up after a few hours.

She injected her mother, kissed her on the forehead, and left, grasping the painted canvases. She headed towards the market and placed all her paintings in the center of the market in the form of a circle. The people of the town were stunned to watch the way Madeline had imprinted art with colors. Despite the appreciation she received, none of her paintings were sold. As it got darker, she took her artwork and left.

The following night, Madeline remained occupied in sculpting extra-ordinary sculptures. Her routine was no different than the previous night. She stopped creating sculptures after the brightness of the sun and dimmed the light of her night lamp. She had stopped going to both her jobs. She knew that if she kept on working that way, she was never going to make enough money to buy medicines for her mother.

The next day, she picked up the paintings and went to the market. She first placed the paintings there and asked one of the shopkeepers to look after them. Since the economic situation was terrible, most of the shops were out of business, which is why every shop owner was more than willing to help. She then returned home and brought the sculptures along. The people were even more fascinated to see the young girl's talent, yet nothing had been sold.

The shop owner, whom she had requested to look after while she was away to fetch the sculptures, offered her to keep her painting in his shop for the night. She agreed and went home to create even more paintings and sculptures. It was her third day in the market, and she was eagerly hoping to earn some money. The news across the town had spread that the young *"statue girl"* had revisited the market with some beautiful art. The news spread rapidly from the town to the small villages and cities located near it. People from different vicinities started visiting the town market, and on the fifth day, her paintings and sculptures began to be sold. She had two more days to buy the medicines as the next dosage was supposed to be given after twelve days. On the sixth day, the market was full of tourists and visitors.

Madeline's every painting and sculpture was sold. She had made enough money that she could buy the medicines. She even paid some money to the shop owner who had helped her with making the sales. The profit was amazing. She spent the same night, creating both sculptures and paintings on the canvas. The response on the seventh day was no different than the previous day. The people who visited the market from different towns not only bought what

Madeline was selling but also bought various products from other shops. It improved the business of the town and restored financial stability. The Mayor of the town managed to convert a few tourists into investors, and over the course of a few weeks, the town prospered. The Mayor was on the verge of selling the local heritage when Madeline revamped the market by attracting tourists through her inspirational art.

Everybody who saw the paintings and sculptures felt calm, and at peace, by merely viewing the masterpieces Madeline had created. The Mayor came to visit Madeline and witnessed the art himself when the word reached to him that a young girl was doing wonders with art. He said that Madeline was the reason behind the town's recovery. He even bought a few paintings for his house.

Madeline was satisfied that she was able to buy the medications with ease but continued to be worried about her mother's health, who was still in a comma. She had earned enough that she could buy the medicines for the next few months, but for her, it was not the money which was important since all her happiness lay in her mother's recovery.

Chapter 10
Calling

The evil power could not bear how things were re-stabilizing. It had never been easy for the evil power to manipulate people, causing them to distort the peace of society. The evil power miserably failed in creating barriers in Madeline's path to acquire the gifts from the Guardian. It had already lost to the Guardian in almost every aspect, and Madeline was going to continue the legacy of the evil power did not do something soon. Madeline had grown into a beautiful woman.

She had become a responsible and civilized woman from a young wild girl. Madeline, herself never realized the transition as her situation had thoroughly consumed her. To Madeline, life was all about ensuring Karen received her medications timely. Besides her mother, there was nothing else that interested her. Unbeknownst to Madeline, she had embraced all the gifts bestowed by the Guardian upon her. She had mastered the art of painting and sculpting amazing sculptures. It is said that artists have to be vulnerable.

Only then are they able to bring out the true creativity that lies within them. Madeline, as a 25-year-old, had experienced different dimensions of her life. Unfortunately, most of her experiences had tragic endings associated with them. Madeline was always a sensitive girl, somebody who was still willing to help others without looking for any personal gains. Madeline truly deserved to be the chosen one, and so, she was.

The evil power decided to bring unrest in the town. This time around, the turmoil projected was to be the worst of all. The evil was committed to turning the town into such a miserable place that nobody living there was to remain safe. The evil power had, on a few occasions, managed to turn the people of the town against each other, but every time Madeline brought them together through the art-making abilities the Guardian had gifted her.

The evil power knew that the people of the town were close to each other and did not have the temperament to bear hatred in their hearts for a long time. The evil power knew the next set of members he was going to manipulate was not going to be the residents of the town. The evil power planned to convince the wildest and cruelest robbers of the region to rob the town. Since the town was economically prospering, he figured that re-drawing them back into the situation from where Madeline had rescued them would indeed be an ideal start. It was not going to be easy to convince the robbers to expand their territory. Robbers usually stayed where they were and preferred robbing people who passed by the village where they resided. The evil, disguised as a traveler, moved from between the town in the middle of the night to maximize its chances of being robbed.

He disguised himself as an older man, pretending to be somebody who was just passing by. However, he was intercepted by the robbers as soon as he entered their territory. The robbers surrounding the evil power were glad to find a bag in the older man's hand, which was full of gold coins. The robbers asked the older man where he was from. The evil power masked as a business merchant lied that he was a citizen of the town where Madeline lived.

The older man began telling the robbers about how rich the people of his town were. The group of robbers consisted of seventy men. Not all of them agreed to the idea of traveling a hundred miles away in search of gold. However, the majority amongst them was so amazed to see the gold coins that they were immediately convinced and began preparing for their trip to the place the older man had told them about.

The people of the town were busy with their daily routines, not knowing what storm was heading their way. The seventy robbers planned to hit the city and stay there until they robbed every single coin of gold. Although the town's financial situation had improved, the town was far from wealthy. However, the fierce period of famine and poverty was over, and most citizens were quickly able to provide for themselves and their families.

The bandits assumed they were going to become the richest ones of their kind. They had robbed enough from the older man that it was enough to pay for all their travel expenses. The evil power knew that when the robbers would realize the town was not a rich one, which would trigger them in such a way that they would start attacking the people of the town and destroy everything they could in their power.

Also, being unaware of the real financial situation, the hunt for the gold coins would force them to rob every person that lived in the town. By then, Madeline had a straightforward routine. She never returned to her old jobs but instead used her paintings to pay for her expenses. She would earn enough that she would easily purchase medicines for her mother. After breaking up with her boyfriend, she never met somebody the same way she had met Mark. Madeline would be working most of the day without having any interaction with anybody besides the people she worked for. Apart from work, the only people she met were the doctors. When Madeline began selling her masterpieces in the market, she had no interest in her customers except for them buying what she was offering to sell.

It had been a few days since the bandits set off for Madeline's town. The day of their arrival had come. The robbers entered the city and killed the guards policing the boundaries. They began robbing as many people as they could, but none of them showed any signs of having gold coins. Most of the people had silver coins, which were the currency of the region, and as the evil power had planned, the robbers were not at all pleased.

News had spread that the robbers had broken into the town. Ironically, they were called *"The Army of Knights."* They were given this title because of the body armor they wore. The men were exceptional riders who had reached the town on their horses. All of them were tall with long beards and swords. They did not have any guns and the way they fought; it became evident that they did not need any.

Just like everyone else, Madeline had also heard about the Army of Knights. She was not as terrorized by them as the others. She grew curious to see them. Madeline had lost any hopes in having any gifts even though the gifts were the only reason Karen had survived, and Madeline had made it this far.

Not everyone in the town had witnessed the robbers, and neither did anyone know where they lived. The evil power had guided them to a place in the woods, which was unknown to many people of the village. The robbers would rob the houses at night and return to the woods before daylight. They would slaughter anyone who tried to resist or react. The police were unable to stop them, and the streets of the town stood vacant in terror.

After a few days, when the robbers realized that none of the residents owned any gold coins, they grew outrageous. They had not traveled over a hundred miles for anything. They had dreamt of being wealthy, and the disappointment had made them extremely angry. Soon they began destroying public property. They went into the market and burnt down most of the shops. When they reached the market, Madeline was also present there. She looked at the robbers and was astonished to witness the muscular men destroying everything in their range. The people in the market began running in an attempt to save their lives. Madeline, in the chaos, stood still and was amused to see how these men were burning down the shops. One of the robbers realized that in the chaos, a beautiful young girl was the only one who did not panic. Madeline did not know how she was so patient. The robber approached the area where Madeline had placed her paintings and sculptures. He smiled at Madeline, a smile that was not pleasant but rather horrific.

He struck one of the sculptures with the sword that instantly perished it with the strike. He then set fire to the paintings, and that is when Madeline jogged home, constantly turning back and establishing eye contact with the man for short intervals. The robber also maintained the eye contact without diverting his attention to the panic he and his associates had brought.

Madeline returned home in a confusing state. She did not know why she was not as scared as the other people around her. Even then, one of the robbers could kill her at any moment. She did not experience fear for a fraction of a second. Madeline returned home and began speaking to her mother, who Madeline believed heard everything she said. Karen, in comma, did not give her any responses, but Madeline knew she could hear. She told Karen how the Army of Knights had caused chaos in the market and how they had been robbing the people of their town. *"I didn't feel scared, and I feel like I have forgotten what fear feels like."* She took a pause and looked at her mother. She then continued, *"Maybe I could sense that the robbers aren't bad people. They need our help."* She realized that Karen was in no position to help. She corrected her statement, *"Well, I guess my help would do it."*

Madeline began telling her mother how she had established eye contact with one of the robbers, and despite his aggressive attitude, through his eyes, she felt that he was a vulnerable man. If anyone had any ears to Madeline's one-sided conversation would have assumed her to have lost her sanity, but these traits in her personality were all polished by the Guardian. What she had observed was indeed true. Madeline began thinking about the purpose of her life. She was neither sad nor distressed that all her hard work was burnt down. She knew all she had to do was create another piece of art. She had stored enough medicines for Karen that they were sufficient to last for the entire year, so there was not much she had to be worried about.

The talent in her art was the only thing that motivated her to live. The incident at the market had made her re-think her goals and her past. The doubt did not just appear in her mind. The Guardian had made her ponder over her past and present. It had created a void in her heart, which could only fulfill her destiny once identified. Madeline, for the first time, attempted to speak to the Guardian. Never had she ever so firmly believed in the Guardian and its influence. Even though she had gained confidence in the fact that she had been receiving help from the Guardian and that there was a purpose behind the guidance. She had to prove to herself that she had not lost her mind.

She began to speak, *"Are you here, around me?"* Madeline said it in a loud voice and then began swirling her head to look around if somebody was there. *"If you truly exist, show yourself to me. "* Madeline was starting to grow nervous. She knew the same light she had witnessed in her dreams could eliminate the darkness of her sorrows. She looked around everywhere but found nothing to be changed, let alone finding the light. Drowning in discomfort, Madeline lay down next to her mother and began focusing on the ceiling of the room. She rejected any further thoughts on the matter and forced her mind to stop thinking about it. She closed her eyes to force herself into sleep, but that did not turn out to be helpful either. She opened her eyes again, in an anger-fueled by anxiety, when suddenly she noticed the room was illuminated. She instantly sat up straight and followed the light, which led her into the room where she painted and sculpted monuments. As soon as she stepped in, she heard a voice – the same voice she had heard years ago.

"You have been protected and guided throughout your life. You did not need the guidance to survive; you needed it to shine. My child, you are the chosen one. You have to maintain peace and fight oppression. You have to be righteous and combat the deceitful. You have to make this world a better place. Evil can never end, but it can be restricted. I, the Guardian, have chosen you to carry the

legacy, and from now on, you have to ensure that the world remains at peace. You have it in you, Madeline, you always had. Pick up the canvas and use your powers. The town needs you."

The voice disappeared, and so did the light. Madeline was astonished. She had received all the answers she had been searching for. She knew what her purpose in life was. She immediately picked up her canvas and began magically used the colors – the same way she had before. Madeline placed the canvas on the floor, and within moments, got lost in painting it. She painted a beautiful picture of the sun as if it was emitting rays of prosperity and happiness.

She placed the canvas on one side and then began sculpting a design. She kept on designing it till it got bright. She did not know anything about the state of the streets, nor did she care. She completed her sculpture and carried it to an old heritage building along with the painting. She placed the sculpture on the entrance gate of the old heritage building. Holding the canvas in her hand inwards, she made sure no one could see the painted side. The streets of the village were empty. People were scared to step out of their houses because of the robbers. The robbers' next target was burning down the old heritage structure, and when they approached it to destroy it, they were surprised to find a young girl guarding the structure with no weapons, but a sculpture. As the robbers got close, they were awestruck to see the sculpture. It seemed as if a human did not create it. They stared at the statue for a while, feeling as if they had frozen. On that visit, there were not seventy men, but rather there were seventy-one. The evil power accompanied them, disguised as another knight.

The sculpture was so amazing that the robbers and the evil power surrendered. They placed their weapons on the floor and kneeled to the statue. The people of the village noticed the men prostrating before the sculpture, and soon, the entire town stood outside the old heritage building. The new Guardian had embraced her powers, and the evil power was defeated. The security and peace of the town restored yet again – this time without any possibilities of its destruction since the evil, too, had surrendered. Madeline returned home after a while and found Karen was out of her comma. She ran to her mother and hugged her tightly. Karen knew that the baby in the cradle would save the town one day. It was a 25 years long journey, and in the end, as always, the good defeated the evil. The lessons we learn in life have a meaning associated with them. At that moment, we might not be able to relate to what the future awaits us, and that curiosity drives us to strive for new beginnings. While Karen and Madeline rejoiced their union, a little girl was climbing the stairs of Madeline's doorway. She knocked when she reached the front door, and Madeline turned toward the door as soon as she heard it.

When Madeline opened it, the girl tightly hugged her and did not even give her an instant to react. Madeline dropped to her right knee in an attempt to talk to the child. Before Madeline could speak, the girl said, *"Please, come save us."* Without giving Madeline any time to pose her questions, the young 10-year-old girl turned around and ran away at a sluggish pace. Madeline stood astounded, staring outside her main door as the little girl disappeared behind the trees.

THE CENTURION

BRANTLEY LOOMIS